Prepared in cooperation with the National Aeronautics and Space Administration

Monitoring Coastal Inundation with Synthetic Aperture Radar Satellite Data

Open-File Report 2011–1208

U.S. Department of the Interior
U.S. Geological Survey

Monitoring Coastal Inundation with Synthetic Aperture Radar Satellite Data

By Yukihiro Suzuoki, Amina Rangoonwala, and Elijah Ramsey III

Prepared in cooperation with the National Aeronautics and Space Administration

Open-File Report 2011–1208

U.S. Department of the Interior
U.S. Geological Survey

U.S. Department of the Interior
KEN SALAZAR, Secretary

U.S. Geological Survey
Marcia K. McNutt, Director

U.S. Geological Survey, Reston, Virginia: 2011

This and other USGS information products are available at http://store.usgs.gov/
U.S. Geological Survey
Box 25286, Denver Federal Center
Denver, CO 80225

To learn about the USGS and its information products visit http://www.usgs.gov/
1-888-ASK-USGS

Suggested citation:
Suzuoki, Yukihiro, Rangoonwala, Amina, and Ramsey, Elijah III, 2011, Monitoring coastal inundation with Synthetic Aperture Radar satellite data: U.S. Geological Survey Open-File Report 2011–1208, 46 p.

Acknowledgments

The research described in this report was supported in part by the National Aeronautics & Space Administration (NASA) under the "Earth and Science for Decision Making: Gulf of Mexico Region" program (NNH08ZDA001N-GULF). Envisat Advanced Synthetic Aperture Radar data are owned by the European Space Agency and were provided via the Cat-1 7286 and 2865 Projects. We thank Rebecca Sanches of NASA's Alaska Satellite Facility, located in the Geophysical Institute of the University of Alaska at Fairbanks, for her kind and indispensable help in the acquisition of data used in this study.

We also acknowledge the invaluable assistance of Thomas H. Cecere of the U.S. Geological Survey's (USGS) National Center in Reston, Virginia, in helping us acquire data for this study. Gratitude is extended to Kari Cretini of USGS for her assistance in accessing water-level data records and to staff of the USGS Lafayette Publishing Service Center for help in preparation of this report.

Contents

Abstract 1

Introduction 1

    Study Area 2

    Study Objectives 3

    Background 3

        The Importance of Strategic Inundation Mapping in Coastal Louisiana 3

        Inundation Mapping with Optical Satellite versus SAR Data 3

        Point Measurements, Hydraulic Models, and Inundation Mapping 3

        Detection of Marsh Subcanopy Flooding by Using SAR 4

        Spatial Coverage Extent Versus Spatial Resolution 4

Methods 5

    Collecting, Calibrating, and Georeferencing Satellite Data 5

        PALSAR and ASAR Scene-Collection Parameters 8

    Collecting Coastal and Inland Hydrologic Data 8

    Assessing Hydrologic Station Locations 8

    Validating SAR Areal Data with Hydrologic Point Data 8

    Mapping Inundation Extents 9

        Selecting a Reference Scene 9

        Delineating Permanent Water Bodies 9

        Determining of Change Detection Thresholds 11

        Inundation Mapping with SAR-based Change Detection 11

Results 11

    Coastal and Inland Water Levels 11

    Inundation Extent Mapping 12

        SAR Reference Scenes 12

        Inundation Thresholds 16

        Assessments of SAR-based Inundation Maps 17

        Influence of Reference-Scene Selection on ASAR-Based Mapping Performance 30

Discussion..30
    Complications of ASAR-Based Inundation Mapping 30
    Visual Comparisons of SAR-based Inundation Maps...35
    Validating SAR-based Inundation Maps with Inland Water-Level Data 35
Conclusion...43
References...43

Figures

1. Map showing study area covering the coastal marshes of Louisiana, as well as locations of nearshore water-level gages monitored by the National Oceanic and Atmospheric Administration 2

2. Diagram of swath coverage provided in generic scenes captured by Synthetic Aperture Radar (SAR) sensors 5

3. Scenes captured by Synthetic Aperture Radar (SAR) sensors, with orbital and look directions included 6

4. Examples of hydrologic stations in the Coastwide Reference Monitoring System that were unsuitable for use in validating Synthetic Aperture Radar-based inundation mapping...9

5. Hydrograph for 2008 dates at Coastwide Reference Monitoring System station 0465 10

6. Monthly mean sea level measurements during 2008 at seven coastal hydrologic stations included in the National Ocean Service's Tides & Currents program...12

7. Map showing locations of hydrologic stations in the Coastwide Reference Monitoring System within the region of the Louisiana coastal zone. Marsh categories are also shown...13

8. Graph depicting sigma-nought change-detection results when comparing inundation across reference-scene and target-scene data obtained by an Advanced Synthetic Aperture Radar (ASAR) sensor aboard the European Space Agency's Envisat 16

9. Inundation maps created from Phased Array type L-band Synthetic Aperture Radar (PALSAR) scenes acquired by the Japanese Aerospace Exploration Agency's Advanced Land Observing Satellite............................17

10. Inundation maps created from Advanced Synthetic Aperture Radar (ASAR) scenes exhibiting horizontal transmit and receive (HH) polarization that were acquired by the European Space Agency's Envisat.....................25

11. Inundation maps created from Advanced Synthetic Aperture Radar (ASAR) scenes exhibiting vertical transmit and receive (VV) polarization that were acquired by the European Space Agency's Envisat...........................28

12. Inundation mapping results derived by using an Advanced Synthetic Aperture Radar (ASAR) target scene acquired on September 17, 2008, by the European Space Agency's Envisat. A comparison of results derived from using two different ASAR reference scenes ispresented 34

13. Change-detection of inundation results compared with water-level measurements at inland hydrologic stations within the Coastwide Reference Monitoring System 36

14. Change-detection of inundation results compared with water-level measurements at inland hydrologic stations within the Coastwide Reference Monitoring System 39
15. Change-detection of inundation results compared with water-level measurements at inland hydrologic stations within the Coastwide Reference Monitoring System 40

Tables

1. Collection date, orbital path, and coverages for scenes acquired by the Phased Array type L-band Synthetic Aperture Radar (PALSAR) sensor aboard the Japanese Aerospace Exploration Agency's Advanced Land Observing Satellite 7
2. Collection date, orbital track, and coverages for scenes acquired by the Advanced Synthetic Aperture Radar (ASAR) sensor aboard the European Space Agency's Envisat 7
3. Landfall dates and times of tropical storms and hurricanes in the Gulf of Mexico, 2006–9...13
4. Mean sea level measurements along the western Louisiana coast corresponding to dates when Phased Array type L-band Synthetic Aperture Radar scenes were acquired during 2007–9 14
5. Mean sea level measurements along the eastern Louisiana coast corresponding to dates when Phased Array type L-band Synthetic Aperture Radar scenes were acquired during 2007–9 14
6. Mean sea level measurements along the western Louisiana coast corresponding to dates when Advanced Synthetic Aperture Radar scenes with horizontal transmit and receive polarization were acquired during 2006–9 15
7. Mean sea level measurements along the eastern Louisiana coast corresponding to dates when Advanced Synthetic Aperture Radar scenes with horizontal transmit and receive polarization were acquired during 2006–9 15
8. Mean sea level measurements along the western Louisiana coast corresponding to dates when Advanced Synthetic Aperture Radar scenes with vertical transmit and receive polarization were acquired during 2007–9 15
9. Mean sea level measurements along the eastern Louisiana coast corresponding to dates when Advanced Synthetic Aperture Radar scenes with vertical transmit and receive polarization were acquired during 2007–9 16
10. Inundation results for the western Louisiana coast compared with water-level measurements at inland hydrologic stations along the Louisiana coast...........................23
11. Inundation results for the eastern Louisiana coast compared with water-level measurements at inland hydrologic stations along the Louisiana coast...........................24
12. Inundation results for the western Louisiana coast compared with water-level measurements at inland hydrologic stations along the Louisiana coast...........................26
13. Inundation results for the eastern Louisiana coast compared with water-level measurements at inland hydrologic stations along the Louisiana coast...............................26

14.   Inundation results for the western Louisiana coast compared with water-level
       measurements at inland hydrologic stations along the Louisiana coast....................................29
15.   Inundation results for the eastern Louisiana coast compared with water-level
       measurements at inland hydrologic stations along the Louisiana coast....................................34

Conversion Factors

SI to Inch/Pound

Multiply	By	To obtain
Length		
centimeter (cm)	0.3937	inch (in.)
meter (m)	3.281	foot (ft)
kilometer (km)	0.6214	mile (mi)
Area		
square kilometer (km²)	0.3861	square mile (mi²)

Monitoring Coastal Inundation with Synthetic Aperture Radar Satellite Data

By Yukihiro Suzuoki,[1] Amina Rangoonwala,[2] and Elijah Ramsey III[3]

Abstract

Maps representing the presence and absence of surface inundation in the Louisiana coastal zone were created from available satellite scenes acquired by the Japanese Aerospace Exploration Agency's Advanced Land Observing Satellite and by the European Space Agency's Envisat from late 2006 through summer 2009. Detection of aboveground surface flooding relied on the well-documented and distinct signature of decreased backscatter in Synthetic Aperture Radar (SAR), which is indicative of inundated marsh in the Gulf of Mexico. Even though decreases in backscatter were distinctive, the multiplicity of possible interactions between changing flood depths and canopy height yielded complex SAR-based representations of the marshes.

Validated by comparison to inland water levels, success of inundation mapping was primarily related to the operational frequencies of the SAR used to perform the mapping. Success of mapping was based on frequency of correspondence between satellite- and ground-based data. Overall, the most successful mapping (83 percent correspondence) was derived from Phased Array type L-band SAR (PALSAR), while mapping derived from C-band Advanced SAR (ASAR) was less successful (≤61 percent correspondence). Exceptions to the low performance of ASAR-based mapping (defined as >76 percent correspondence) occurred when water levels were well below or above ground, occurring over spatially extensive portions of the ASAR scene.

When mapping day-to-day coastal inundation extents, results indicate that SAR systems operating at C-band frequencies are not as effective as those operating at L-band frequencies; however, multiple factors not related to frequency also reduced the effectiveness of C-Band in detecting subcanopy inundation. C-band has performed and continues to perform exceedingly well in applications for response to dramatic events and when strategic collections are available; however, L-band seems to be more suitable for day-to-day mapping of coastal inundation.

Introduction

The use of satellite-based Synthetic Aperture Radar (SAR) to monitor coastal Louisiana inundation was evaluated by the Remote Sensing Applied Research group at the U.S. Geological Survey's (USGS) National Wetlands Research Center. This initial applied research emphasized preparation of flood distribution maps for coastal Louisiana. The research included data collected by the Phased Array type L-band SAR (PALSAR) sensor onboard the Advanced Land Observing Satellite (ALOS) and the Advanced SAR (ASAR) sensor onboard Envisat. This combination of satellite-based SAR sensors provided the maximum temporal frequency of data collections covering the Louisiana coastal zone. An added advantage of the combination was the ability to compare the performance of two widely used SAR sensor systems operating at different frequencies or wavelengths—the L-band PALSAR and the C-band ASAR. SAR systems operating at both L- and C-band frequencies have repeatedly proven capable of mapping inundation in coastal and river floodplain systems.

Even though flood-extent mapping has become a routine and even operational activity in coastal marsh and forested wetland landscapes (Ramsey, 1998, 2005; Lu and Kwoun, 2008), especially during and after extreme storm events, satellite-based observations of long-term effects of flooding on natural vegetation are less common, and the usefulness of such observations requires further study. As reported in Ramsey and others (2009), the combined use of radar imagery (Envisat ASAR) and optical imagery (Landsat

---

[1] Formerly of ASci Corporation, Inc. (McLean, Virginia), for the U.S. Geological Survey (currently of Japan Space Imaging Corporation, Tokyo, Japan)

[2] Five Rivers Services, LLC, for the U.S. Geological Survey

[3] U.S. Geological Survey

Thematic Mapper [TM]) provided synergistic observations to document the extent of the coastal surge accompanying Hurricane Ike (Sept. 13, 2008) and a resultant marsh-dieback event. The dieback could be directly attributed to prolonged water logging and elevated salinity levels. This connection illustrated how inundation monitoring with frequent satellite-based radar data observations, combined with cloud-free optical data, can provide direct linkages between vegetation condition and the primary physical forces controlling it.

Study Area

The study area included coastal wetlands stretching from the western chenier to the eastern deltaic plains[1] of coastal Louisiana, located in the north-central Gulf of Mexico (fig. 1). The deltaic plain was formed and is primarily sustained by the direct deposition of Mississippi River sediments, while the chenier plain is primarily dependent on current-related

[1] The two major regions of the Louisiana coast are the chenier plain in the southwestern region and the deltaic plain in the southeastern region. See Saucier (1994) and Barrow and others (2007, p. 156) for further definitions.

reworking of river sediments from the Atchafalaya River (Coastal Louisiana Ecosystem Assessment & Restoration, 2006). Relationships between water and sediment gave rise to highly permeable sand and shell (cheniers) barriers in the west and barrier islands in the east that protect extensive back barrier marshes that extend inland by 6–24 kilometers (km), commonly at less than 1.5 meters (m) above mean sea level and with slopes of less than 0.2 m per km (Chabreck, 1970).

The Louisiana coastal-marsh zone is dominantly underlain by frequently saturated soils. In this zone, subsurface faulting can produce surface subsidence that results in marsh submergence and fragmentation and, ultimately, the formation of permanent water bodies (Kiage and others, 2005; Morton and others, 2005). In addition, hurricanes scour the marsh, creating small water bodies (Neyland, 2007), and push water with elevated salinity into freshwater marshes, causing salt burn in those areas (Neyland, 2007; Ramsey and others, 2009). Aggravating these detrimental impacts are channels and levies, as well as impounds (constructed to provide transport conduits and waterfowl sanctuaries) that impede overland flow. These impediments can lengthen marsh exposure to elevated salinity water and, in the case of intense

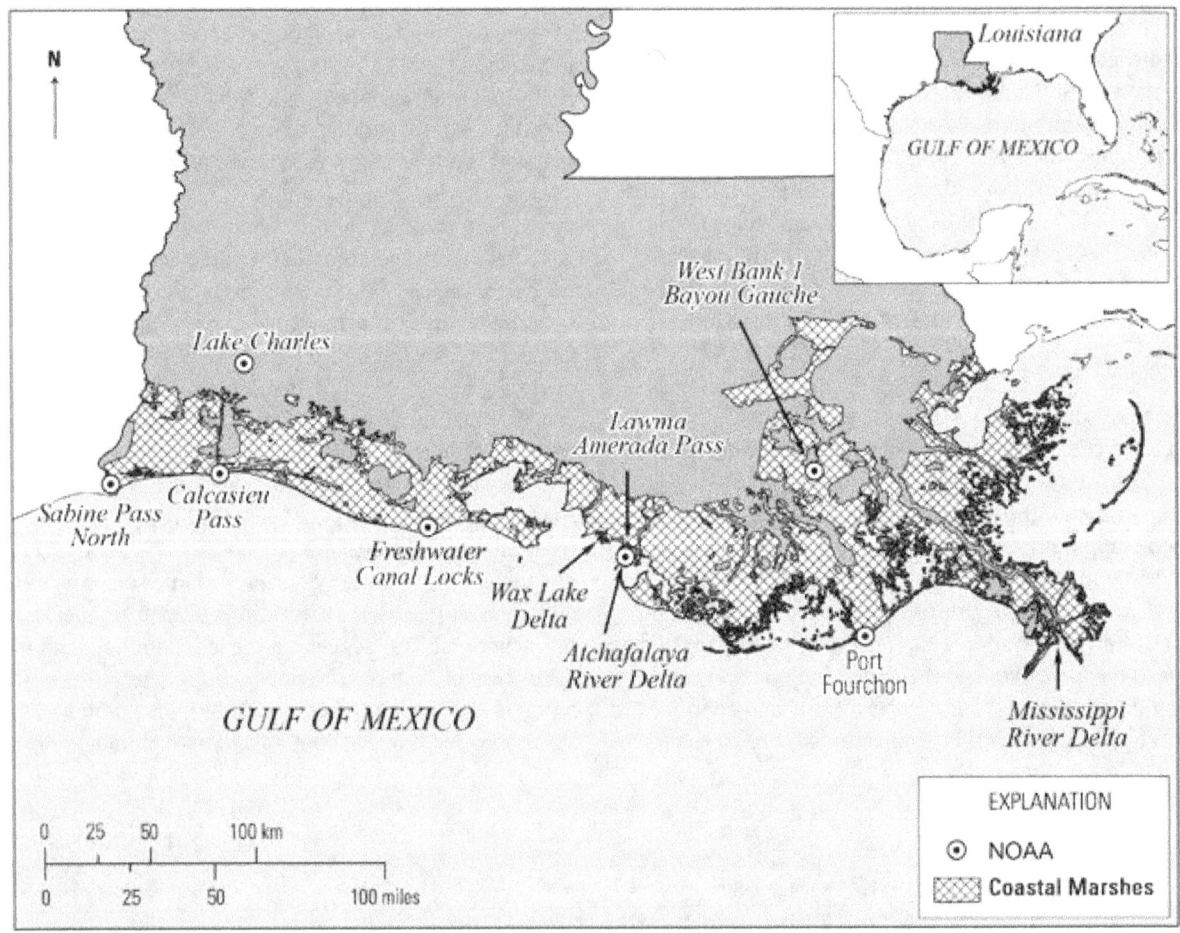

Figure 1.   Map showing study area covering the coastal marshes of Louisiana, as well as locations of nearshore water-level gages monitored by the National Oceanic and Atmospheric Administration (NOAA) (2010).

rainfall accompanying storm events, prolong inundation and promote water logging that can advance marsh alteration and deterioration. The combination of low topographic relief, poorly drained soils, tectonic activity, and flow impedance creates a spatially complex hydrological landscape.

Study Objectives

The goal of our applied research was to demonstrate the ability of SAR-based satellite imagery to monitor the distribution and occurrence of storm-related and tidal-related flooding in Louisiana coastal wetlands. Our demonstration is based on available SAR scenes that individually covered at least half the coastal zone from late 2006 to September 2009 (fig. 1). Research goals included the following: (1) to derive inundation distributions from available SAR scenes, (2) to discover limitations and successes of SAR-based inundation mapping, (3) to assess the Coastwide Reference Monitoring System (CRMS) hydrologic water-level database appropriateness for validation of SAR-based mapping, and (4) to discover implications for continued applied research.

A successful research strategy should be based upon routine measurements that are cost effective and easily implemented into operational resource management. Furthermore, measurements should be verified against and calibrated with available, currently operational ground-based measurements (Nielsen and Werle, 1993).

Background

The Importance of Strategic Inundation Mapping in Coastal Louisiana

The coastal zone of Louisiana, located in the central-northern Gulf of Mexico, accounts for about 40 percent of the coastal tidal wetlands in the continental United States (Neyland, 2007). As in most coastal zones that include expanses of marsh, the zone is depicted by a gradual increase of elevation that starts at sea level at the coast and reaches 1 to 1.5 m at the southern extent of upland prairie and forests. In addition to flood events (Kiage and others, 2005; Ramsey and others, 2009), the seasonal and interannual marsh phenology (Wang, 2004) and the ephemeral nature of many small water bodies (Kiage and others, 2005) in these marshes produce a highly dynamic landscape. In order to precisely identify the threshold duration of saturation required for wetland viability, these dynamics must be accounted for (Lang and others, 2008). While limited results do not allow immediate inferences to be made regarding the health of or trends in the marsh system, evidence suggests that episodic events can cause severe stress on marsh vegetation in the region (Ramsey and others, 2009; Ramsey, Werle, and others, in press).Produced systematically, maps portraying wetland

vegetation condition and spatially distributed inundation can provide crucial information for linking wetland health with flood frequency and duration (Hess and others, 1995; Ramsey, 1995; Werle and others, 2000; Toyra and Pietroniro, 2005).

Inundation Mapping with Optical Satellite versus SAR Data

Passive remote sensing with optical sensors can adequately address many issues of coastal resource management (Klemas and others, 1993; Smith, 1997; Lunetta and others, 1998; Henry and others, 2006); however, map production based on optical systems are critically limited by their dependence on sunlight and favorable weather conditions when time-constrained collections are needed (Hess and others, 1995; Smith, 1997; Ramsey, 1998, 2005; Werle and others, 2000; Toyra and Pietroniro, 2005; Lang and others, 2008). Even when reliance on time-constrained collections is minimized, the restricted penetration of visible and near-infrared radiation into full cover canopies limits detection of subcanopy flooding with optical systems (Ormsby and others, 1985; Moghaddam and others, 2003; Toyra and Pietroniro, 2005).

Remote sensing systems using radar offer a viable alternative data source when timely and consistent collections are needed (Kasischke, 2003; Ramsey and others, 2006; Matgen and others, 2007; Lu and Kwoun, 2008). SAR sensors operating at centimeter-long wavelengths can collect information day and night and in most weather conditions, and they provide increased canopy penetration (Ormsby and others, 1985; Hess and others, 1995; Lewis and others, 1998; Ramsey, 1998; Toyra and Pietroniro, 2005). Satellite-based radar sensors, such as the C-band ASAR aboard the European Space Agency's Envisat, the C-band SAR aboard the Canadian Space Agency's Radarsat, the X-band SAR aboard the German TerraSAR-X, and the PALSAR aboard the Japanese Aerospace Exploration Agency's ALOS, have proven to be valuable tools for surveying land and water surfaces during weather-related emergencies (Committee on Earth Observation Satellites, 2008).

Point Measurements, Hydraulic Models, and Inundation Mapping

Conventional contour mapping by using point measurements of water levels is hampered by the high spatial variability of flood occurrences, difficulties in timing field data collections with highly dynamic flood events, and inherent problems in predicting flood stages in marsh by using off-site gages (Leconte and Pultz, 1991; Ramsey, 1995). Hydraulic flow models can be used to predict inundation patterns (Smith, 1997), alleviating many difficulties inherent in conventional contouring. Nevertheless, lack of the necessary spatial density of stage measurements and the prevalent disconnect between marsh and off-site measured flows diminish the capability to provide calibration and validation of hydraulic models (Werle and others, 2000; Matgen and others, 2007). To help overcome these difficulties in monitoring and simulating the spatially distributed and rapidly changing nature of coastal inundation, remote sensing systems are used.

Detection of Marsh Subcanopy Flooding by Using SAR

Although L-band provides increased canopy transmittance of longer wavelengths, which implies superior mapping of subcanopy inundation (Ramsey, 1998; Kasischke and others, 2003; Toyra and Pietroniro, 2005), C-band has performed well in flood mapping of Louisiana marshes, as it has in other marshes occupying the northern Gulf of Mexico coasts (Ramsey, 1995; Kasischke and others, 2003; Kiage and others, 2005; Ramsey and others, 2009) and elsewhere (Hess and others, 1995). C- and L-band SAR data in horizontal transmit and receive (HH) and vertical transmit and receive (VV) polarizations (acquired by the Shuttle Imaging Radar-C [SIR-C] platform) were used by Pope and others (1997) to demonstrate that flooding of herbaceous vegetations can be exhibited as an increase or decrease in SAR backscatter. In effect, the nature of the change in water level and the ability to differentiate between flooded and nonflooded marshes depend on several biophysical variables, including marsh type, height, density, and stem orientation and size, as well as soil moisture, inundation depth and history, and SAR sensor parameters (Kasischke and others, 2003; Grings and others, 2005; Pope and others, 1997).

In coastal marshes occupying the northern and eastern Gulf of Mexico, the interrelation between biophysical variables and incident C-band SAR signals dominantly produce a decrease in backscatter from flooded versus nonflooded marshes. For example, C-band SAR data with VV polarization, which were acquired by the European Remote Sensing Satellite-1 (ERS-1), indicated that backscatter from flooded marsh was lower than that from nonflooded marsh in the northeastern Gulf of Mexico(data were field validated by Ramsey [1995] and modeled by Dobson and others [1996]). Similarly, while studying a variety of southeastern Gulf of Mexico marshes, Kasischke and others (2003) used C-band SAR data with VV polarization (acquired by ERS-2) to substantiate a progressive decrease in backscatter with increasing flood level and a positive relationship between soil moisture and SAR backscatter. In the north-central Gulf of Mexico, Kiage and others (2005) used C-band SAR with HH polarization (acquired by RADARSAT-1) to document decreased backscatter from hurricane surge-flooded saline, brackish, and fresh coastal marshes, compared to presurge backscatter intensities. Even the TerraSAR X-band system was used to successfully estimate water-level changes in south Florida marshes (Hong and others, 2010). In addition, any polarization influence on the effectiveness of flood mapping (for example, Grings and others, 2005) was expected to favor

the copolarized (VV and HH) SAR data as applied in the current study as compared to cross-polarized (HV [horizontal send, vertical receive] and VH [vertical send, horizontal receive]) SAR data (for example, Smith, 1997). SAR data (HH and VV polarizations) trends for fresh to saline coastal marshes of the northern Gulf of Mexico have consistently indicated an association between decreased backscatter and flooded marshes, as compared to nonflooded marshes.

Spatial Coverage Extent Versus Spatial Resolution

Consistent and sequential (systematic) data collection is required for detecting and quantifying long-term environmental trends for resource monitoring and short-term dramatic change for emergency response. The frequency of data collection determines if the dynamics of the feature of interest are either captured or missed (Klemas, 2005). For instance, coastal resource phenologies should preferably be captured on a weekly basis, and coastal flooding should be captured every 2 h or better (Klemas, 2005). A 2-h revisit frequency is not feasible with any operational satellite system; however, if systematic sampling is available, higher frequency sampling may be approximated (Hager and others, 2009). For example, linking the tidal excursion (inland extent) to the flood stage over a single tidal cycle is an unreasonable observational requirement for orbiting satellites. If, however, the collections occur weekly or bimonthly over a long period of time, the tidal stages and excursions at the times of each collection may be aggregated to construct a series of tidal excursion extents that simulate a much higher collection frequency over a single tidal period. To obtain a reasonable hypsometric simulation, a bimonthly or better collection frequency is desired.

There is a tradeoff between spatial resolution and repeat frequency (for example, Schaber and Badeck, 2003; Fisher and Mustard, 2007). In essence, the higher the temporal frequency of scene captures, the coarser the ground spatial resolution. For example, large-format SAR collections made at bimonthly to weekly or higher repeat frequencies primarily provide moderate spatial resolutions (for example, 150 m or less) (Hager and others, 2009). In addition to high reoccupation frequency, large-format satellite coverages provide a synoptic and regional collection perspective and continuity to the coastal inundation mapping. Regional and frequent SAR collections coupled with similar collections of optical satellite data promote the early detection of adverse regional impacts, improving the opportunity of remediation before irreparable loss of the coastal resource (Hager and others, 2009). In fact, research has shown that high-frequency collections at higher spatial scales (for example, 25 m or less), even in contiguous landcovers, can obscure the detection of change (for example, Schaber and Badeck, 2003; Fisher and Mustard, 2007).

Higher signal variability accompanying higher spatial resolution data could lower change-detection performance by concealing real differences within the signal noise (spatial variability). As will be discussed, scanning systems such as radar aggravate the issues related to spatial resolution and change-detection performance because of their dependency upon signal and scan angle, factors that can cause the appearance of change irrespective of whether the target changed or not. Because a greater number of high spatial resolution scenes are required to cover an extensive region (for example the entire Louisiana coastal zone), dependency upon the signal and scan angle is intensified relative to scenes acquired at lower spatial resolution but having greater regional coverage.

While large-format monitoring provides a regional synoptic view, allows for rapid response, and promotes early detection of change, modes having a moderate swath (for example, 60 km) and higher spatial resolution have advantages as well. Such modes afford stand-level canopy information necessary for determining features such as the following: (a) the underlying wetland function, (b) canopy structures (for example, canopy gaps, subcanopy size, and species-type distributions), and (c) regeneration of and shifts in coastal wetland-species associations in response to storms, flooding, herbivory, fires, and climate changes (Hager and others, 2009). Because of the performance issues related to spatial scale and change-detection performance previously discussed, higher

spatial resolution scenes would be most appropriately used to better define and mediate problems in the change-detection performance; while present in the regional scale products, such problems cannot be properly identified or examined at the coarser spatial resolution (Ramsey, Spruce, and others, in press).

Methods

Collecting, Calibrating, and Georeferencing Satellite Data

SAR coverages were acquired by the PALSAR sensor aboard ALOS and the C-band ASAR sensor onboard the Envisat. PALSAR scenes were collected in Wide Area Observation mode (Burst Mode 1 [WB1]) at a nominal spatial resolution of 100 m and incidence angles of 18° in the near-range to 43° in the far-range of the imaged swath (fig. 2). All PALSAR scenes used in this study were collected in the descending orbital direction (fig. 3A; table 1). To allow scene-to-scene comparability, PALSAR scenes with HH

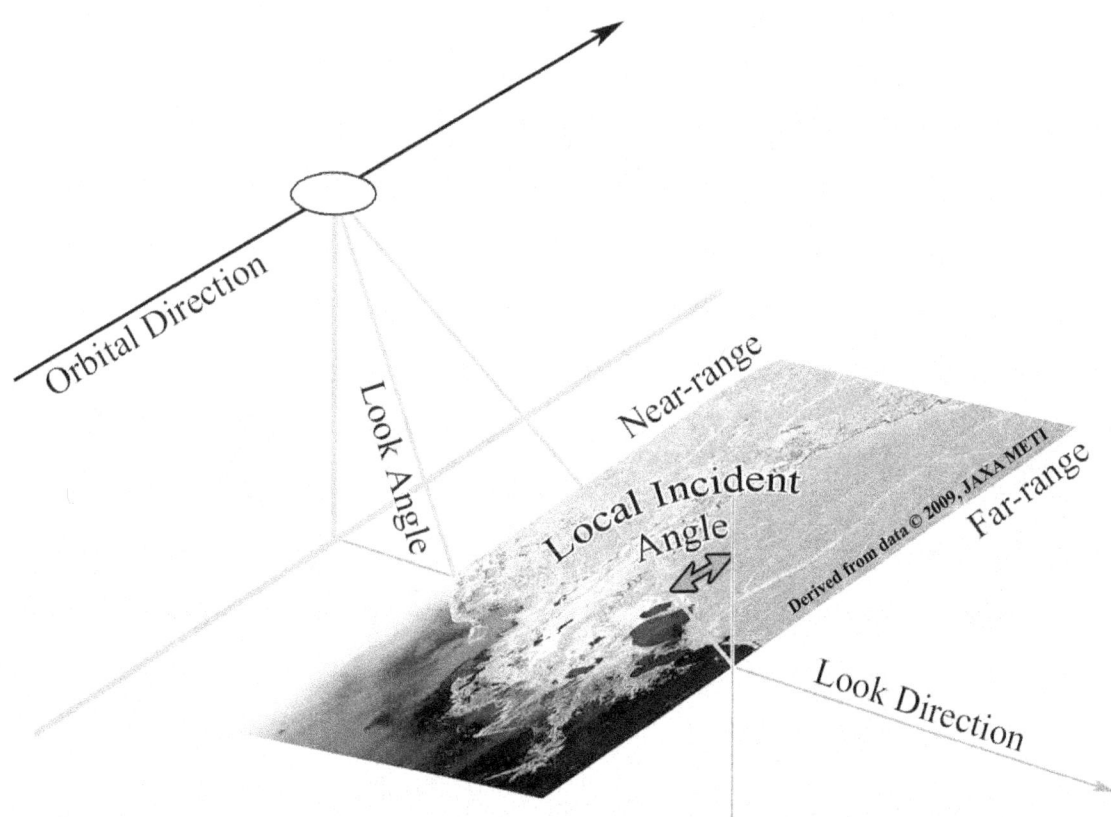

Figure 2.   Diagram of swath coverage provided in generic scenes captured by Synthetic Aperture Radar (SAR) sensors. The example scene included in the diagram was captured by a Phased Array type L-band SAR sensor aboard the Japanese Aerospace Exploration Agency's Advanced Land Observing Satellite. Orbital and look directions, look and local incident angles, and near range and far range are illustrated.

(horizontal send and receive) polarization were radiometrically calibrated to the sigma naught backscattering coefficient (σ_o) with remote sensing software available at the Alaska Satellite Facility Website (2010). The 21 PALSAR scenes selected from January 2007 through September 2009 included all PALSAR scenes collected over coastal Louisiana (fig. 3*A*; table 1).

The C-band ASAR scenes were collected in Wide Swath mode at a nominal spatial resolution of 150 m and incidence angles of 17° in the near-range to 42° in the far-range of the imaged swath. The ASAR scenes were collected in both the ascending and descending orbits that had a variety of look directions (figs. 3*B,C*; table 2). ASAR scenes with HH and VV polarizations were transformed to σ_o estimates by using Next ESA SAR Toolbox (NEST) software and calibration coefficients provided by the European Space Agency (European Space Agency, 2007). The 24 ASAR scenes selected were collected from July 2006 to September 2009, and their times of collection corresponded to a wide range of sea levels and tidal flushing (figs. 3*B,C*; table 2).

All SAR data were registered to a Landsat Thematic Mapper (TM) Lambert Conformal Conic (LCC) base image having 25-m spatial resolution. Using the LCC projection eliminated problems due to the presence of multiple Universal Transverse Mercator (UTM) zones, and the LCC matched the State Plane Coordinate system for Louisiana. The LCC projection (WGA84 geoid) used two standard parallels separated by 1.5° latitude, a central meridian, and a false northing and easting defined by the State Plane Coordinate system for southern Louisiana. Applying State Plane parameters, we found that areas projected in the LCC and in Albers Equal Area Conic (AEAC) differed by <0.01 percent. In addition, the LCC base was assessed by comparison to direct USGS Digital Orthophoto Quarter Quadrangles (DOQQs). Rectification errors of the LCC base to the DOQQs were most often less than 0.5 pixels. Registration errors of the LCC base to all satellite-based SAR scenes ranged between 0.2 and 0.5 pixels.

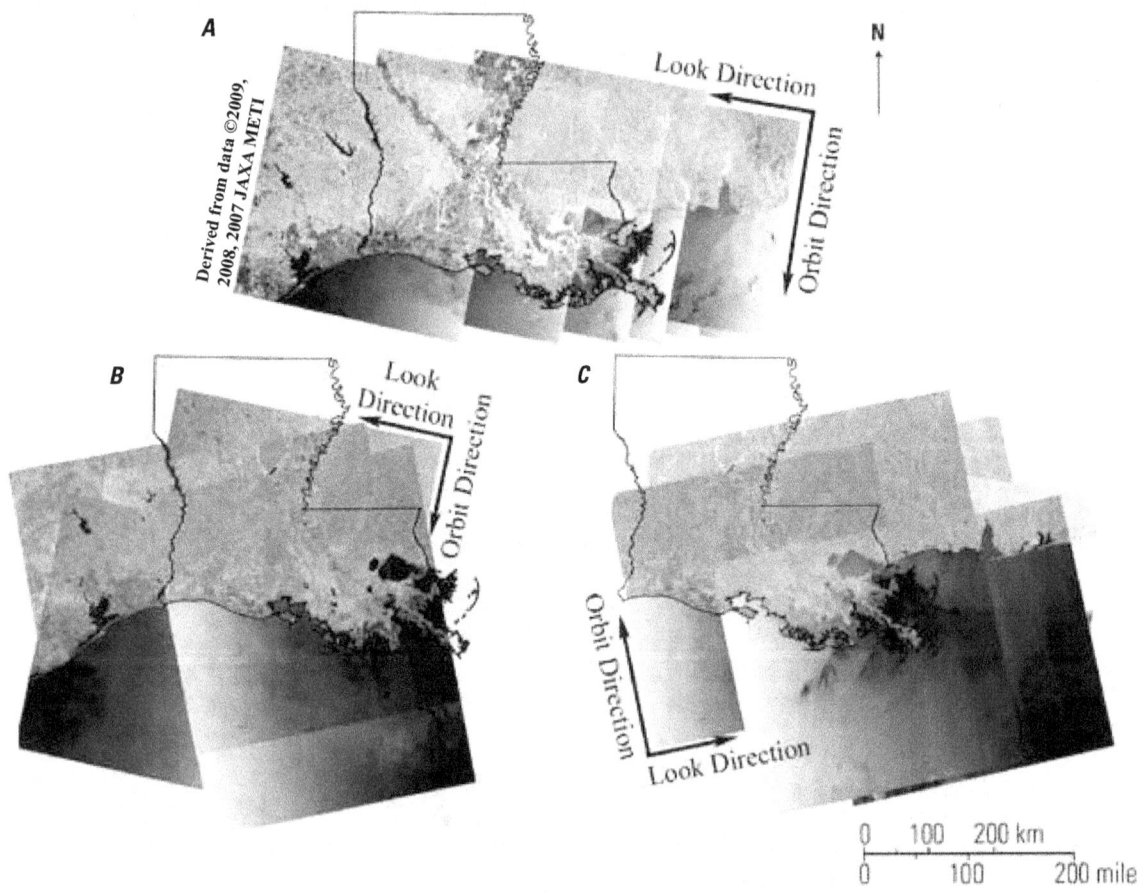

Figure 3.   Scenes captured by Synthetic Aperture Radar (SAR) sensors, with orbital and look directions included. *A*, Scenes captured by the Phased Array type L-band SAR (PALSAR) sensor aboard the Japanese Aerospace Exploration Agency's Advanced Land Observing Satellite (ALOS; derived from data ©2009, 2008, 2007 JAXA METI). *B*, Western region; scenes acquired by the Advanced Synthetic Aperture Radar (ASAR) sensor aboard the European Space Agency's Envisat. *C*, Eastern region; scenes acquired by the ASAR sensor aboard Envisat. All ALOS PALSAR data are descending orbit (from north to south), western look direction. Envisat ASAR data are mixed with both descending orbit and ascending orbit (from south to north) and eastern and western look directions.

Table 1. Collection date, orbital path, and coverages for scenes acquired by the Phased Array type L-band Synthetic Aperture Radar (PALSAR) sensor aboard the Japanese Aerospace Exploration Agency's Advanced Land Observing Satellite (ALOS). PALSAR scenes were collected in Wide Area Observation Mode (Burst Mode 1 [WB1]).

[Path, ALOS PALSAR apparent path over ground; coverage refers to the region of the Louisiana coastal zone covered by the scene]

Date	Path	Coverage	Date	Path	Coverage
	2007			2008	
Jan. 7	487	East	Jan. 10	487	East
Jan. 12	490	West	Jan. 15	490	West
Feb. 22	487	East	July 24	485	East
July 10	487	East	Sept. 8	485	East
July 15	490	West	Sept. 25	486	East
Aug. 25	487	East	Oct. 7	484	East
Aug. 30	490	West		2009	
Oct. 10	487	East	Jan. 12	487	East
Oct. 15	490	West	Jan. 17	490	West
Nov. 25	487	East	Jan. 22	493	West
Nov. 30	490	West	Sept. 16	488	East

Table 2. Collection date, orbital track, and coverages for scenes acquired by the Advanced Synthetic Aperture Radar (ASAR) sensor aboard the European Space Agency's Envisat. ASAR scenes were collected in Wide Swath mode.

[Track, Envisat ASAR apparent path over ground; Pol., polarization; HH, horizontal transmit and receive; VV, vertical transmit and receive; coverage refers to the region of the Louisiana coastal zone covered by the scene]

Date	Track	Coverage	Pol.
	2006		
Jul. 27	[1]434	West	HH
	2007		
July 25	[1]119	East	HH
July 31	[1]205	West	HH
Sept. 4	[1]205	West	VV
Sept. 14	[1]348	East	VV
	2008		
July 28	[1]391	East	VV
Aug. 3	[1]477	West	VV
Aug. 29	[1]348	East	VV
Sept. 1	[1]391	East	VV
Sept. 1	[2]398	West	VV
Sept. 14	[2]83	West	VV
Sept. 17	[1]119	East	VV
	2009		
Mar. 11	[1]119	East	VV
Mar. 30	[1]391	East	HH
Apr. 2	[1]434	West	HH
May17	[2]83	West	VV
May20	[1]119	East	VV
May20	[2]126	West	VV
May23	[1]162	Central	VV
May27	[2]226	West	VV
June 24	[1]119	East	HH
June 27	[1]162	West	HH
Aug. 30	[2]83	West	VV
Sept. 12	[2]269	East	VV

[1]Scenes captured in ascending orbital mode.

[2]Scenes captured in descending orbital mode.

PALSAR and ASAR Scene-Collection Parameters

The look and orbit directions were constant for all PALSAR scenes used in the inundation analyses (fig. 3A). Look-angle ranges were constant, and swath ranges were similar in PALSAR scenes covering the eastern and western regions (figs. 2 and 3A). In contrast, the ASAR scenes exhibited a high variety of orbit and look directions, look-angle ranges, and swath ranges (figs. 3B, C). Also in contrast to the PALSAR scenes, the ASAR scenes exhibited noticeably higher intensities in the near-range and a progressive decrease in intensities extending towards the far-range. Finally, ASAR scene polarizations varied between HH and VV, in contrast to the constant HH polarization of the PALSAR scenes. Comparability of the ASAR scenes was hindered by these variables, which also impeded the performance of ASAR-based mapping of subcanopy inundation.

Collecting Coastal and Inland Hydrologic Data

Records of coastal water-level timing and height were obtained for seven coastal hydrologic stations from the National Ocean Service's Tides & Currents program (National Oceanographic and Atmospheric Administration, 2010). These are located along the eastern (Port Fourchon, West Bank1, Bayou Gauche, Freshwater Canal Locks and Lawma, Amerada Pass), and western (Sabine Pass North, Calcasieu Pass, Lake Charles, Freshwater Canal Locks [overlap]) regions of the Louisiana coast (fig. 1).

Inland water-level data for calibrating and validating the inundation maps were obtained from the Strategic Online Natural Resources Information System (SONRIS, 2009) from the Louisiana Department of Natural Resources. Hydrologic stations used for water-level measurements are included in the Coastwide Reference Monitoring System (CRMS). On December 1, 2009, we received a list of 212 hydrologic stations that were recommended by USGS personnel associated with the CRMS program (G. Steyer and G. Snedden, written commun.).

Stations included on the list had been confirmed to contain the best hydrologic records available for our inundation mapping. Before initiating the final phase of our mapping, we assessed these records. Our criteria included the following: (1) water-levels were referenced to the surrounding marsh surface (marsh ground-surface reference at 0-m) and (2) records displayed continuity and reliability of data. Continuity of data was exhibited by the station having continuous records over the study period, and reliability was expressed by the nature of the data through time. For instance, if the water-levels became near constant for a continued time period, recordings at that site became suspect and were compared to other inland sites. If the suspect records were abnormal when compared to those for other sites, the station was excluded.

Assessing Hydrologic Station Locations

The location of many inland hydrograph stations did not allow direct comparison between recorded water-levels and SAR-based calculations of surface inundation. Although locations on the marsh platform were preferred, most sites were located in water channels that exhibit different flow dynamics than those of the marsh platform and were separated from the marsh platform by varying distances and obstructions, such as levies (fig. 4A-D). Many sites were located in a landscape of mixed marsh and forest stand (fig. 4A and B) or were located in degrading marsh containing a high proportion of open water (fig. 4C–D). In many cases, direct validation of SAR-based flood mapping against hydrologic data was, thus, prevented by problems deriving from the decoupling of measured water levels from flooding occurring within the marsh platform and from the contamination of the SAR pixel by mixed nonmarsh land covers. Practically, in the most egregious cases this incompatibility required removal of sites or adjustment of the assessment location to an area as close as possible to the water-level recording location but within marsh exhibiting the necessary extent and uniformity. If moved, the assessment location was contained totally or partially within 100 or 150 m of the water-level recording site. Even though most hydrologic stations were unsuitable for direct validation of our SAR data, the occurrence or absence of elevated water levels at the remaining stations provided an indication of flooding in the surrounding marshes, and thus, a measure of the performance of our SAR-based flood detection.

Validating SAR Areal Data with Hydrologic Point Data

In general, the comparability of image products that are composites of spatially integrated ground elements (pixels of 100 and 150 m in this case) with point measurements (water-level recorder locations) can be an issue (for example, Fisher and others, 2006; Fisher and Mustard, 2007). This is true aside from specific issues regarding the unsuitability of some of the hydrologic station locations initially selected for our study. This incompatibility between different kinds of data may diminish the reliability of the assessment method, particularly when applied to highly dynamic situations (such as surge flooding and recession in complex marsh systems) occurring in heterogeneous environments. Alternatively, accurately determining surface flooding, particularly when surface-water levels are low (that is, <10 cm), requires fine resolution of data (for example, water-level recordings and average ground-surface elevations of marsh). The combined requirement of acquiring highly accurate ground-surface and water-level elevations and the need for accurate functioning of the water-level recorder may also limit the validity of the point measurements. In the case of this study, invalidity of the point measurements would decrease the perceived reliability of the SAR-based inundation products. In order to help

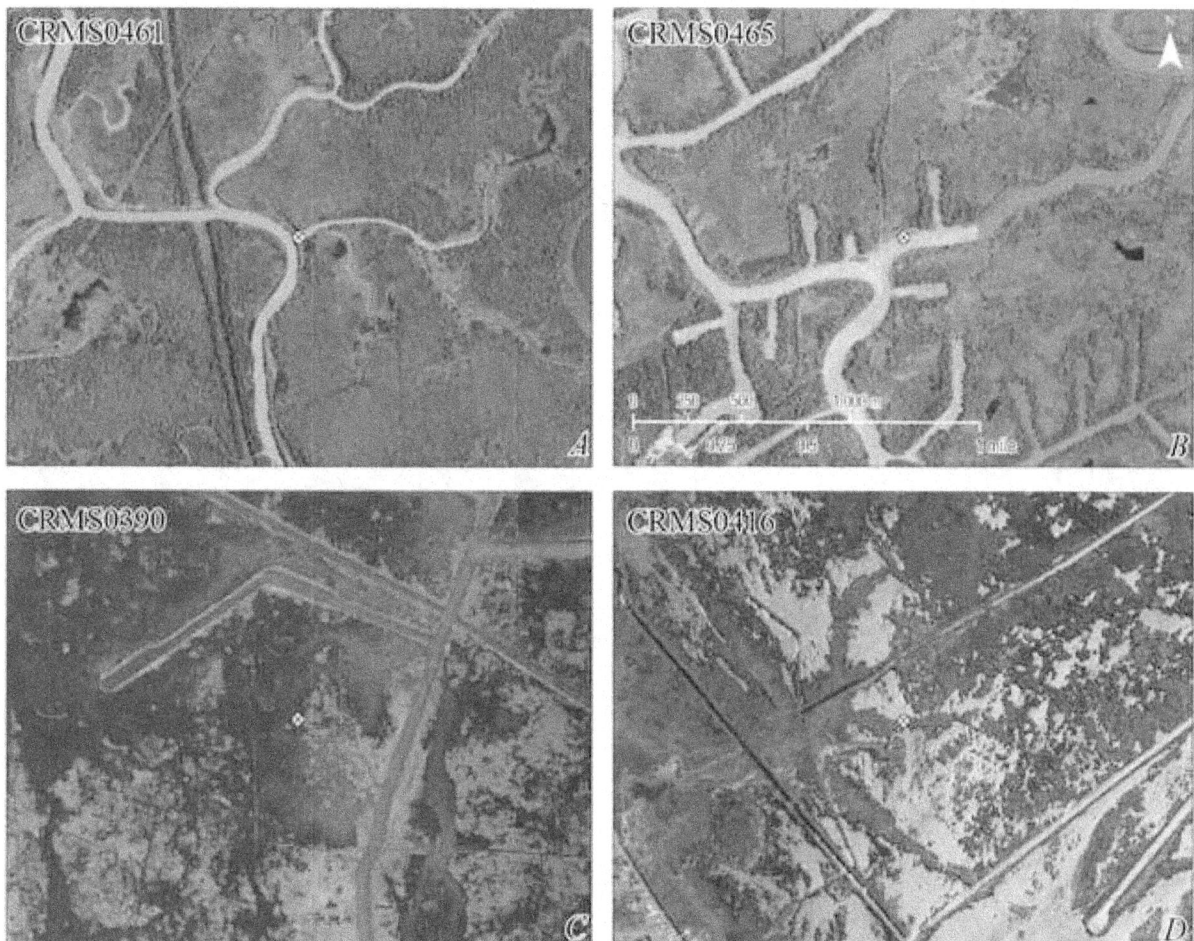

Figure 4. Examples of hydrologic stations in the Coastwide Reference Monitoring System (CRMS) that were unsuitable for use in validating Synthetic Aperture Radar-based inundation mapping. CRMS station identification is provided in the lower right corner of each example. *A, B,* Sites where forests and shrubs were evident within marsh areas. *C, D,* Degraded and largely open-water sites.

improve the calibration and validation of the inundation maps by using inland water-level recordings, we inspected marsh areas adjacent to and surrounding hydrologic stations. These searches were limited to a 100-m (for PALSAR data) or 150-m (for ASAR data) radius surrounding hydrologic stations, within nominal ground resolutions. If there was a high density of flood occurrences within the pertinent 100- or 150-m radius, we concluded the site was flooded.

Mapping Inundation Extents

Selecting a Reference Scene

To successfully validate our ability to detect change related to subcanopy flooding, we preferred to use a reference scene with limited or no flooding and soil water contents at less than saturated levels (Ramsey, 2005, 2008). When choosing reference scenes, we sought to avoid collection

times that were closely following rain events, periods of atypically elevated sea levels (for example, Hurricane Dolly and Tropical Storm Edouard [fig. 5]), or during high tides (for example, spring tides). Additionally, SAR scenes used for reference were chosen as best as possible within the same season to minimize backscatter differences due to variations in vegetation phenology and canopy structure (Ramsey and others, 1999, 2004). These criteria for reference-scene selections helped ensure that our process of inundation mapping best captured subcanopy flooding.

Delineating Permanent Water Bodies

In order to minimize confusion between wind-roughened water surfaces, flooded marsh, and nonflooded marsh, permanent water bodies were defined within the study area (Ramsey and others, 1994; Ramsey, 2005, 2008).The locations and extents of permanent inland water bodies obtained from the Louisiana Oil Spill Coordinator's Office (LOSCO) (2007)

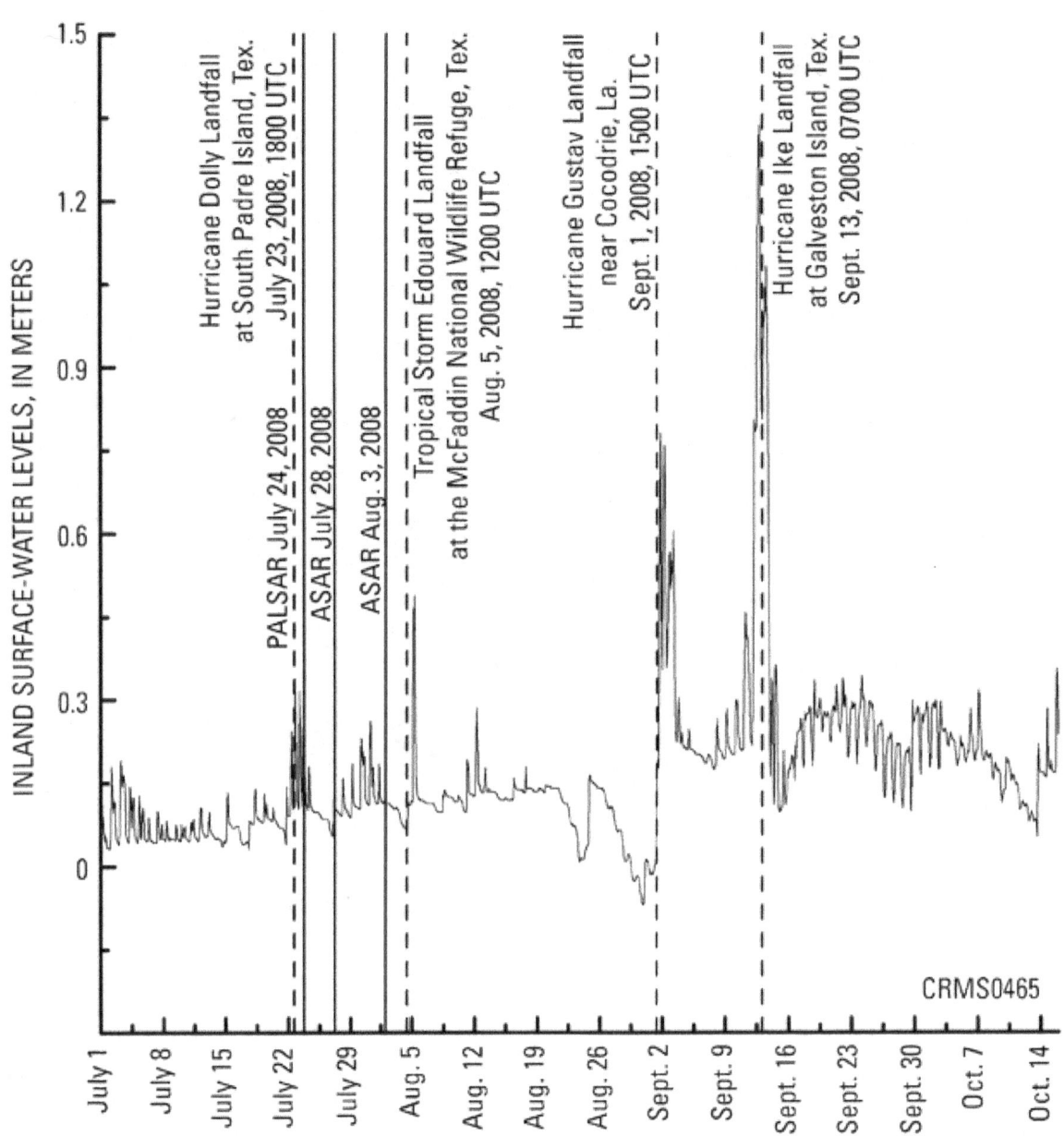

Figure 5. Hydrograph for 2008 dates at Coastwide Reference Monitoring System (CRMS) station 0465 (as noted in fig. 4, this site was not used for inundation validation because mixed vegetation surrounded the site). Acquisition dates for Phased Array type L-band Synthetic Aperture Radar (PALSAR) and Advanced Synthetic Aperture Radar (ASAR) scenes are also provided. Abnormally high sea levels were associated with the impacts of Hurricanes Gustav and Ike and also with the passages of Hurricane Dolly and Tropical Storm Edouard. The influence of these storms on the water levels along the Louisiana coast impeded the ability to select SAR reference scenes appropriate for use in the inundation-change analyses. See table 3 for a list of storms influencing sea level off the Lousiana coast from 2006 to 2009.

were updated with thirteen TM images collected from 2006 to 2008 (western region: June 4, 2006; April 20 and August 10 and 26, 2007; February 18, March 5, and July 27, 2008; central region: June 13, 2006, April 29, 2007, and June 18, 2008; eastern region: June 6, 2006, April 6, 2007, and July 13, 2008) before Hurricane Gustav made landfall on September 1, 2008. These TM images were registered to the same LCC-projected TM-base image used to register SAR scenes. LOSCO open-water polygon coverage was superimposed on the suite of TM images, and the areas of omission between the vector coverage and water bodies on the TM images were determined. Water bodies visually identified on the suite of TM images were at least 40 square kilometers (km^2) in area and exhibited spatial and temporal consistency through 2006 and 2008. These water bodies were classified as permanent water bodies and added to the LOSCO open water polygon coverage. The combined water polygon coverage was used to exclude all permanent water bodies from the SAR-based detection of inundation. In addition, a coastal-extent vector was used to exclude offshore waters (Louisiana Oil Spill Coordinator's Office, 2007). Location errors in the coastal vector were found in association with rapidly changing and spatially complex deltaic marshes, such as in the bird's foot of the Mississippi River Delta, the Atchafalaya River delta, and the Wax Lake delta.

Determining Change Detection Thresholds

To validate our SAR-based inundation maps, we needed to establish minimum inundation thresholds corresponding with reasonable predictions of flooded and nonflooded areas during "normal" conditions. The processing procedure to determine a minimum threshold for detecting reasonable changes in inundation was not an automated one and relied on operator intervention and judgment to determine the threshold (Ramsey, Werle, and others, in press). In principle, this procedure required consideration of radar parameters for imaging flooded and nonflooded terrains as well as background knowledge of flood condition and behavior within a specific geographic setting; both aspects were brought to bear in an informed trial-and-error procedure to determine the extent and configuration of flooded versus nonflooded boundary lines. We checked threshold flood extents for consistency by completing three steps, including the following:

1. by comparing inundation-change results with the original SAR data,

2. by comparing results with the closest date of TM-detected and inland-measured water levels, and

3. by categorizing the terrain over a wide area by either oversaturating or undersaturating the imagery in such a way that known high ground was definitively excluded from contiguous "flooded" pixels and known low-lying, flood-prone areas were included.

Inundation Mapping with SAR-based Change Detection

In order to successfully detect changes related to flooded marsh, each SAR scene was paired with a reference scene having the same HH or VV polarization in order to eliminate change artifacts associated with polarization differences. Calibrated SAR scenes were then subjected to a change-detection algorithm that incorporated an internal, 5 by 5-pixel Kuan speckle filter to dampen noise while preserving edges and shape and retaining spatial continuity of detected inundation (Ramsey, Werle, and others, in press). A logarithmic ratio of the reference and the target scene data resulted in a measurement of decibel difference. A positive decibel difference indicated lower intensities in the target SAR scene, compared to those of the reference scene. If in excess of the predetermined threshold value, the difference was considered indicative of possible inundation. Once appropriate threshold values were obtained, inundation extents were mapped corresponding to the times at which SAR collections were made along the entire Louisiana coast.

Results

Coastal and Inland Water Levels

At all seven coastal hydrologic stations (Strategic Online Natural Resources Information System, 2009; National Oceanic and Atmospheric Administration, 2010), high sea-level variability was recorded from east to west along the Louisiana coast (fig. 6A–G). Many instances of elevated sea levels could be associated with the passage and impacts of tropical storms and hurricanes that occurred in the gulf from January 2006 to January 2010 (table 3). Elevated sea states prevailed in 2007 and 2008 and were more prominent in the eastern portion of the coast than in the western region. Consistently elevated sea levels in 2007 and 2008, particularly in the spring to fall months, made it difficult to select reference SAR scenes that did not exhibit surface flooding or saturated marsh soils.

Of the 212 CRMS hydrologic stations chosen for our study, only 67 were considered acceptable to validate the SAR-based inundation maps. Of these 67 stations, 12 were selected in the western region (fig. 7A) and 14 in the eastern region (fig. 7B) to provide adequate spatial dispersion for validation analyses. For these selected stations, there were comparatively consistent and reliable hydrologic records, and the stations were fairly well distributed across the coast at locations near areas of reasonably contiguous marsh without numerous trees or shrubs. Even though the selected stations represented a good validation set, their locations and associated water-level records were not without glitches that affected their comparability with SAR-based inundation

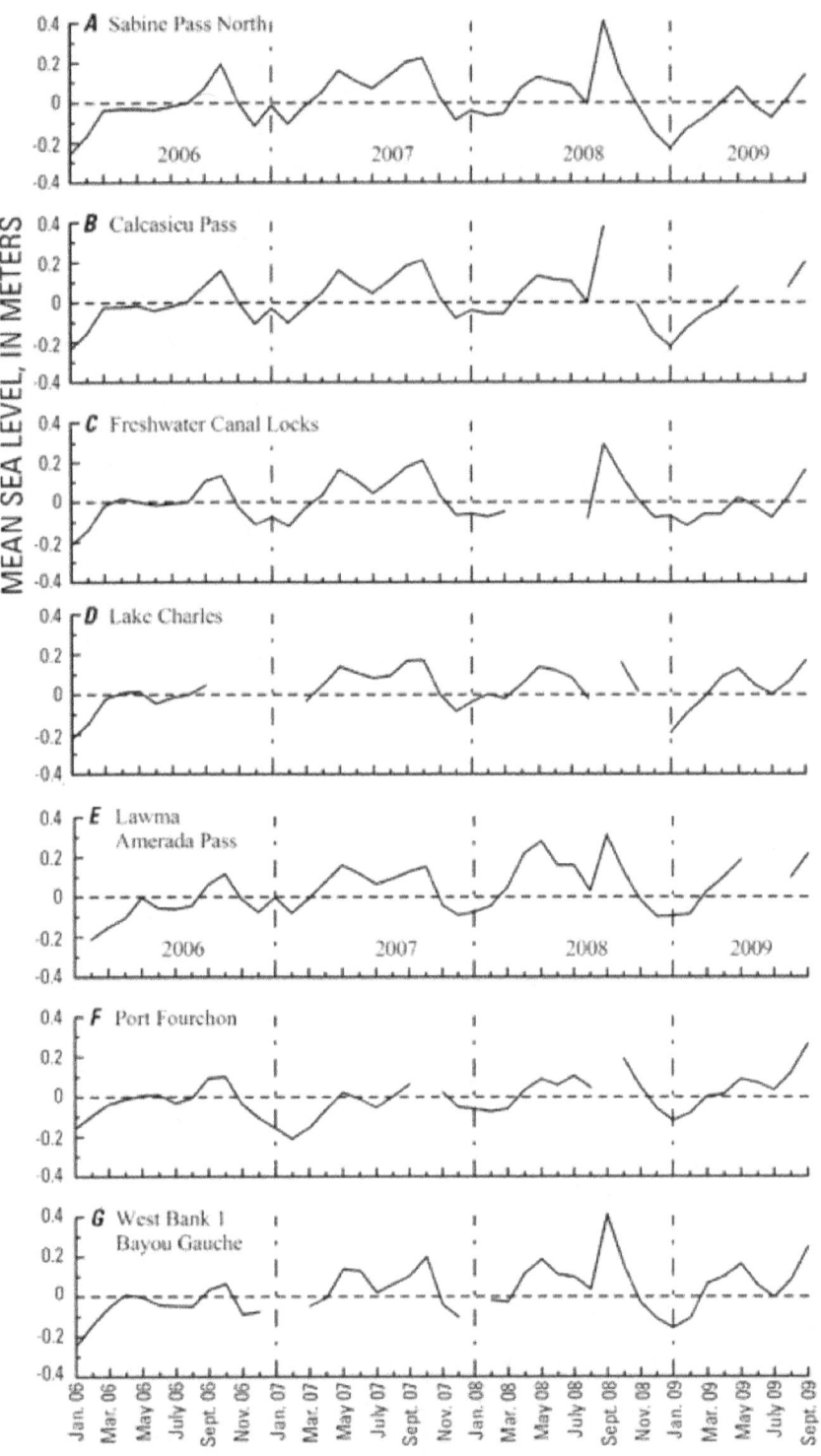

Figure 6.   Monthly mean sea level measurements during 2008 at seven coastal hydrologic stations included in the National Ocean Service's Tides & Currents program (National Oceanic and Atmospheric Administration, 2010). *A*, Sabine Pass North. *B*, Calcasieu Pass. *C*, Freshwater Canal Locks. *D*, Lake Charles. *E*, Lawma, Amerada Pass. *F*, Port Fourchon. *G*, West Bank 1, Bayou Gauche. See tables 4–9 for water levels at times when Synthetic Aperture Radar scenes were acquired.

mapping (see examples of unusable hydrologic stations in fig. 4).

As discussed in the Methods section, incompatibility between the point water-level recording and the SAR inundation mapping and other factors led to using a 100- or 150-m radius centered on the hydrograph point location to confirm the presence or absence of flooding. This spatially expanded criterion of correspondence was most often applied in the eastern region where change-detection results indicated scattered pockets of persistent flooding.

Inundation Extent Mapping

SAR Reference Scenes

For reasons already discussed, selection of SAR scenes for use as reference was complicated by a number of factors. In general, the choice of ASAR reference scenes was more challenging than that of PALSAR reference scenes. After extended comparisons, the best and most consistent selection criteria for reference scenes included the following: (1) scenes needed to correspond to the lowest coastal (tables 4–9) and inland water levels at the highest number of hydrologic stations in the eastern and western regions, (2) reference and target scenes needed to have the same HH and VV polarization, and (3) scenes needed to represent the dominant seasonality of the target scenes. Coastal water levels associated with PALSAR and ASAR reference scenes are included in tables 4–9. Our reference-scene selection criteria most often allowed us to avoid detecting abnormal inundations but did not follow our preference for seasonal correspondence very well. These simple criteria, however, did provide a simulation of operational inundation mapping with satellite-based SAR, where the luxury to carefully scrutinize every detail involved in the reference-scene selection most often does not exist.

Table 3. Landfall dates and times of tropical storms and hurricanes in the Gulf of Mexico, 2006–9.

[UTC, Coordinated Universal Time; NWR, National Wildlife Refuge]

Year	Date	Name	Landfall
2006	June 10–14	Tropical Storm Alberto	0000 UTC June 13, near Apalachicola, Fla.
2007	Aug. 15–17	Tropical Storm Erin	1030 UTC Aug. 16, San Jose Island, Tex.
	Sept. 12–14	Hurricane Humberto	0700 UTC Sept. 13, McFaddin NWR, Tex.
2008	July 20–25	Hurricane Dolly	1800 UTC July 23, South Padre Island, Tex.
	Aug. 3–6	Tropical Storm Edouard	1200 UTC Aug. 5, McFaddin NWR, Tex.
	Aug. 15–26	Tropical Storm Fay	1900 UTC Aug. 21, Flagler Beach, Fla. (3rd landfall)
	Aug. 25–Sept. 4	Hurricane Gustav	1500 UTC Sept. 1, Cocodrie, La.
	Sept. 1–14	Hurricane Ike	0700 UTC Sept. 13, Galveston Island, Tex.
	Oct. 6–7	Tropical Storm Marco	1200 UTC Oct. 7, Misantla, Mexico
2009	Aug. 16–17	Tropical Storm Claudette	0530 UTC Aug. 17, Fort Walton Beach, Fla.
	Nov. 4–10	Hurricane Ida	1800 UTC Nov. 9, Mississippi River, La. to Ala.

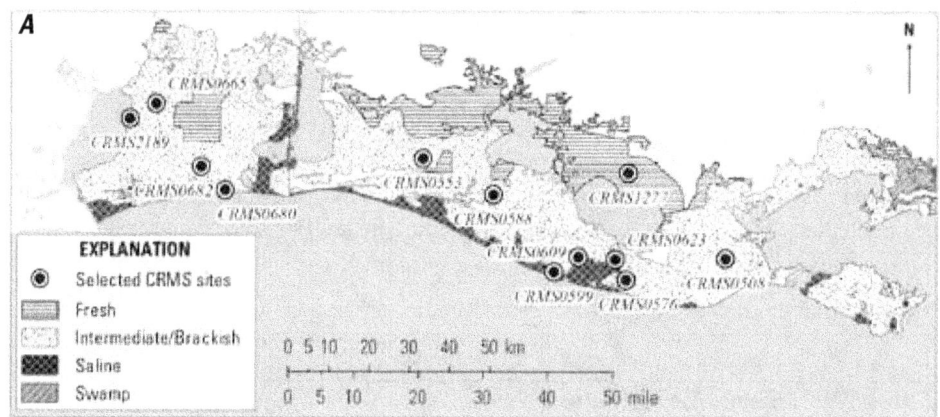

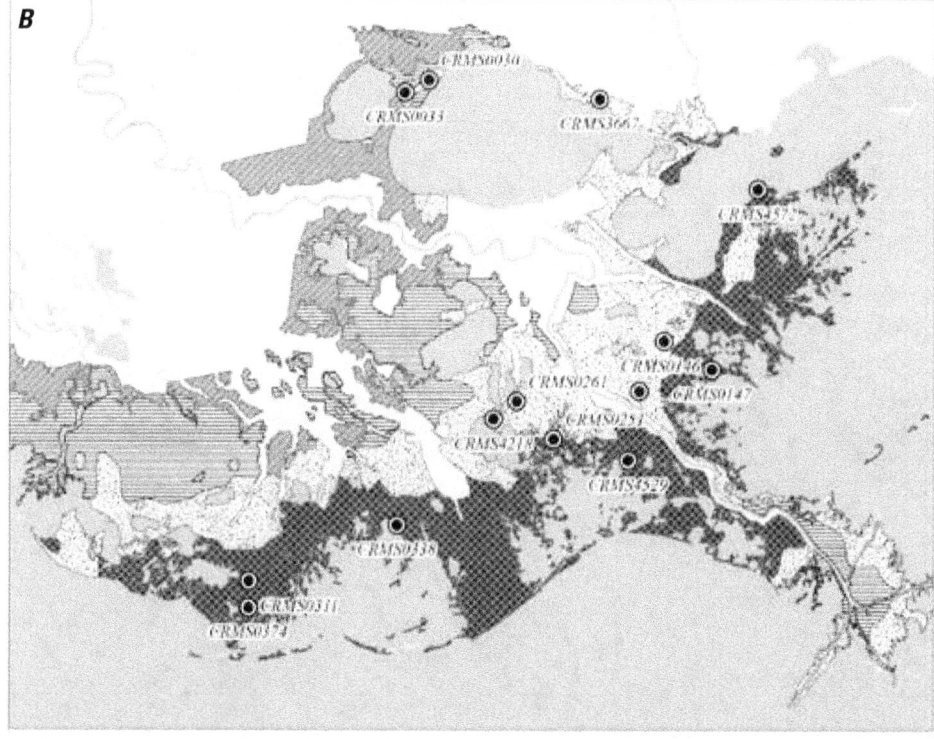

Figure 7. Map showing locations of hydrologic stations in the Coastwide Reference Monitoring System (CRMS) within the region of the Louisiana coastal zone. Marsh categories are also shown (Sasser and others, 2008). *A*, Western region. *B*, Eastern region.

Table 4.   Mean sea level measurements along the western Louisiana coast (see fig. 1; National Oceanographic and Atmospheric Administration, 2010) corresponding to dates when Phased Array type L-band Synthetic Aperture Radar (PALSAR) scenes were acquired during 2007–9.

[Sea level measurements are provided in meters. Measurements corresponding to acquisition of PALSAR data are highlighted in orange. The PALSAR reference scene had a horizontal transmit and receive polarization. PALSAR data were obtained by the Japanese Aerospace Exploration Agency's Advanced Land Observing Satellite]

| Year | Date | Western Coastal Region | | | |
		Sabine Pass North	Calcasieu Pass	Lake Charles	Freshwater Canal locks
2007	Jan. 12	0.083	0.167	-0.038	0.122
	July 15	.233	.190	.291	.184
	Aug. 30	-.023	-.124	.110	-.085
	Oct. 15	.061	-.066	.267	.056
	Nov. 30	-.080	-.218	-.053	-.214
2008	Jan. 15	-.053	-.051	-.257	-.009
2009	Jan. 17	-.153	-.117	-.336	.191
	Jan. 22	-.474	-.383	-.463	-.183
	Oct. 20	-.183	-.270	.156	-.256

Table 5.   Mean sea level measurements along the eastern Louisiana coast (see fig. 1; National Oceanographic and Atmospheric Administration, 2010) corresponding to dates when Phased Array type L-band Synthetic Aperture Radar (PALSAR) scenes were acquired during 2007–9.

[Sea level measurements are provided in meters. Measurements corresponding to acquisition of PALSAR data are highlighted in orange. The PALSAR reference scene had a horizontal transmit and receive polarization. PALSAR data were obtained by the Japanese Aerospace Exploration Agency's Advanced Land Observing Satellite]

| Year | Date | Eastern Coastal Region | | | |
		Freshwater Canal locks	Lawma, Amerada Pass	Port Fourchon	West Bank 1, Bayou Gauche
2007	Jan. 7	-0.262	-0.132	-0.245	0.120
	Feb. 22	-.061	.021	-.082	-.205
	Jul. 10	.132	.204	-.024	.016
	Aug. 25	.329	.259	.228	.136
	Oct. 10	.288	.155	.189	.243
	Nov. 25	-.414	-.325	-.171	-.034
2008	Jan. 10	-.375	-.286	-.191	.056
	July 24	.400	.165	.093	.161
	Sept. 8	.252	.157	.204	.271
	Sept. 25	.420	.282	.358	.321
	Oct. 7	.065	.172	.159	.286
2009	Jan. 12	-.694	-.326	-.372	-.150
	Sept. 16	.295	.433	.412	.356

Table 6.   Mean sea level measurements along the western Louisiana coast (see fig. 1; National Oceanographic and Atmospheric Administration, 2010) corresponding to dates when Advanced Synthetic Aperture Radar (ASAR) scenes with horizontal transmit and receive polarization were acquired during 2006–9.

[Sea level measurements are provided in meters. Measurements corresponding to acquisition of ASAR data are highlighted in orange. ASAR data were obtained by the European Space Agency's Envisat. A, ascending orbital mode]

			Western Coastal Region			
Year	Date	Mode	Sabine Pass North	Calcasieu Pass	Lake Charles	Freshwater Canal locks
2006	July 27	A	-0.054	-0.243	0.336	-0.113
2007	July 31	A	-0.361	-0.452	0.047	-0.502
2009	Mar. 30	A	-0.486	-0.610	0.002	-0.692
	Apr. 2	A	0.186	0.130	0.363	0.167
	Jun. 27	A	-0.158	-0.219	0.177	-0.340

Table 7.   Mean sea level measurements along the eastern Louisiana coast (see fig. 1; National Oceanographic and Atmospheric Administration, 2010) corresponding to dates when Advanced Synthetic Aperture Radar (ASAR) scenes with horizontal transmit and receive polarization were acquired during 2007–9.

[Sea level measurements are provided in meters. Measurements corresponding to acquisition of ASAR data are highlighted in orange. ASAR data were obtained by the European Space Agency's Envisat. A, ascending orbital mode]

			Eastern Coastal Region			
Year	Date	Mode	Freshwater Canal locks	Lawma, Amerada Pass	Port Fourchon	West Bank 1, Bayou Gauche
2007	July 25	A	0.088	-0.050	-0.010	-0.064
2009	Mar. 30	A	-.692	-.199	-.269	.294
	Jun. 24	A	-.642	-.170	-.278	.008
	Jun. 27	A	-.340	-.028	-.053	.075

Table 8.   Mean sea level measurements along the western Louisiana coast (see fig. 1; National Oceanographic and Atmospheric Administration, 2010) corresponding to dates when Advanced Synthetic Aperture Radar (ASAR) scenes with vertical transmit and receive polarization were acquired during 2007–9.

[Sea level measurements are provided in meters. Measurements corresponding to acquisition of ASAR data are highlighted in orange. ASAR data were obtained by the European Space Agency's Envisat. A, ascending orbital mode; D, descending orbital mode]

			Western Coastal Region			
Year	Month	Mode	Sabine Pass North	Calcasieu Pass	Lake Charles	Freshwater Canal locks
2007	Sept. 4	A	0.142	0.200	-0.172	0.053
2008	Aug. 3	A	-.424	-.454	.063	-.431
	Sept. 1	D	-.195	-.447	.095	-1.132
	Sept. 14	D	1.178	.721	.046	.593
2009	May 17	D	.113	.077	-.101	.106
	May 20	D	.215	.279	.046	.209
	May 23	A	-.030	.051	-.018	.011

Table 9.   Mean sea level measurements along the eastern Louisiana coast (see fig. 1; National Oceanographic and Atmospheric Administration, 2010) corresponding to dates when Advanced Synthetic Aperture Radar (ASAR) scenes with vertical transmit and receive polarization were acquired during 2007–9.

[Sea level measurements are provided in meters. Measurements corresponding to acquisition of ASAR data are highlighted in orange. ASAR data were obtained by the European Space Agency's Envisat. A, ascending orbital mode; D, descending orbital mode]

			Eastern Coastal Region			
Year	Month	Mode	Freshwater Canal locks	Lawma, Amerada Pass	Port Fourchon	West Bank 1, Bayou Gauche
2007	Sept. 14	A	-0.050	0.107	0.106	0.200
2008	July 28	A	.101	.116	.080	.025
	Aug. 29	A	-.180	-.243	-.098	.000
	Sept. 1	A	-.101	-.143	.241	.045
	Sept. 17	A	-.111	.027	.322	.574
2009	Mar. 11	A	-.017	-.049	.070	.081
	May 20	A	.193	.150	.155	.056
	May 23	A	.011	.074	.223	.174
	May 27	D	.236	.448	.391	.198
	Aug. 30	A	.202	.062	.162	.132
	Sept. 2	A	-.178	-.233	.022	.052

Inundation Thresholds

In the results of the change-detection analyses used to map inundation distribution in the target scenes, the range and distribution of reference- and target-scene backscatter differences did not exhibit multimodal features but fairly continuous Gaussian-type distributions (an example is shown in fig. 8). This consistency in the analysis of reference and target SAR scenes has been noted previously (Ramsey and others, 2011). It is important to note that differences exhibited in the Gaussian distribution did not include permanent water bodies, as identified in our prechange-detection processing.

As discussed in the "Methods" section, in order to minimize errors of commission (inclusion of nonflooded marshes) and omission (exclusion of flooded marshes) in SAR-based mapping, we used alternate data sources (for example, TM) to select appropriate inundation thresholds. Multiple thresholds were tested for each set of PALSAR and ASAR scenes covering the eastern and western regions of the coast. In the case of PALSAR scenes, all with HH polarization, a threshold value of 2.0 was chosen from a range of threshold values ranging from 1.5 to 2. After extensive testing, a threshold value of 1.0 for scenes with HH polarization was found to best reproduce the inundation patterns validated by our comparison of reference and target SAR scenes. For scenes exhibiting VV polarization, threshold values of 0.1 for the eastern region and 1.0 for the western region were deemed most appropriate.

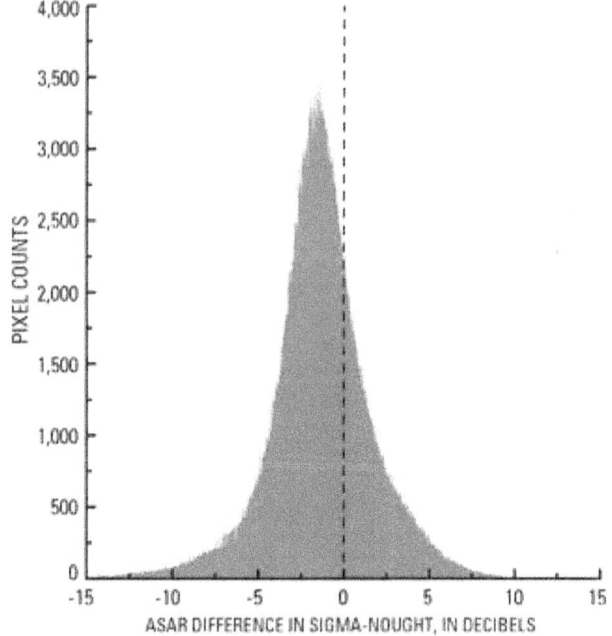

Figure 8.   Graph depicting sigma-nought change-detection results when comparing inundation across reference-scene (acquired July 28, 2008) and target-scene data (acquired September 14, 2008) obtained by an Advanced Synthetic Aperture Radar (ASAR) sensor aboard the European Space Agency's Envisat. Notice the highly Gaussian shape, with only a lightly positive skew, and the lack of any suggested bimodal or multimodal features.

Assessments of SAR-based Inundation Maps

Inundation maps were produced (fig.9A, B) by using calibrated SAR scenes (along with pertinent reference scenes) collected from 2006 to 2009 that were subjected to the inundation-detection procedure. PALSAR-based inundation mapping exhibited good correspondences with coastal and inland water-level data. Correspondence rates of PALSAR-based maps were 83 percent in the western region and 85 percent in the eastern region (tables 10–11). In contrast, correspondence rates of ASAR-based maps were lower and more varied in comparison to PALSAR-based maps.

For the western coastal region, ASAR-based inundation mapping that used scenes with HH polarization yielded a correspondence rate of 53 percent (fig. 10A; table 12) when compared to the coastal and inland water-level data. In the eastern region, the correspondence rate increased to 81 percent (table 13); however, the three ASAR scenes with HH polarization were collected at times when coastal and inland water-level data indicated an absence of flooding throughout the eastern coastal region (fig. 10B).

For the western coastal region, ASAR-based inundation mapping by using VV polarization yielded a correspondence rate of 61 percent when compared to coastal and inland water-level data. This correspondence rate included scenes acquired on September 14, 2008 (associated with high water-levels from storm surge) and August 3, 2008 (associated with regions of spatially extensive tidal or rainfall flooding) (fig. 11A, table 14).

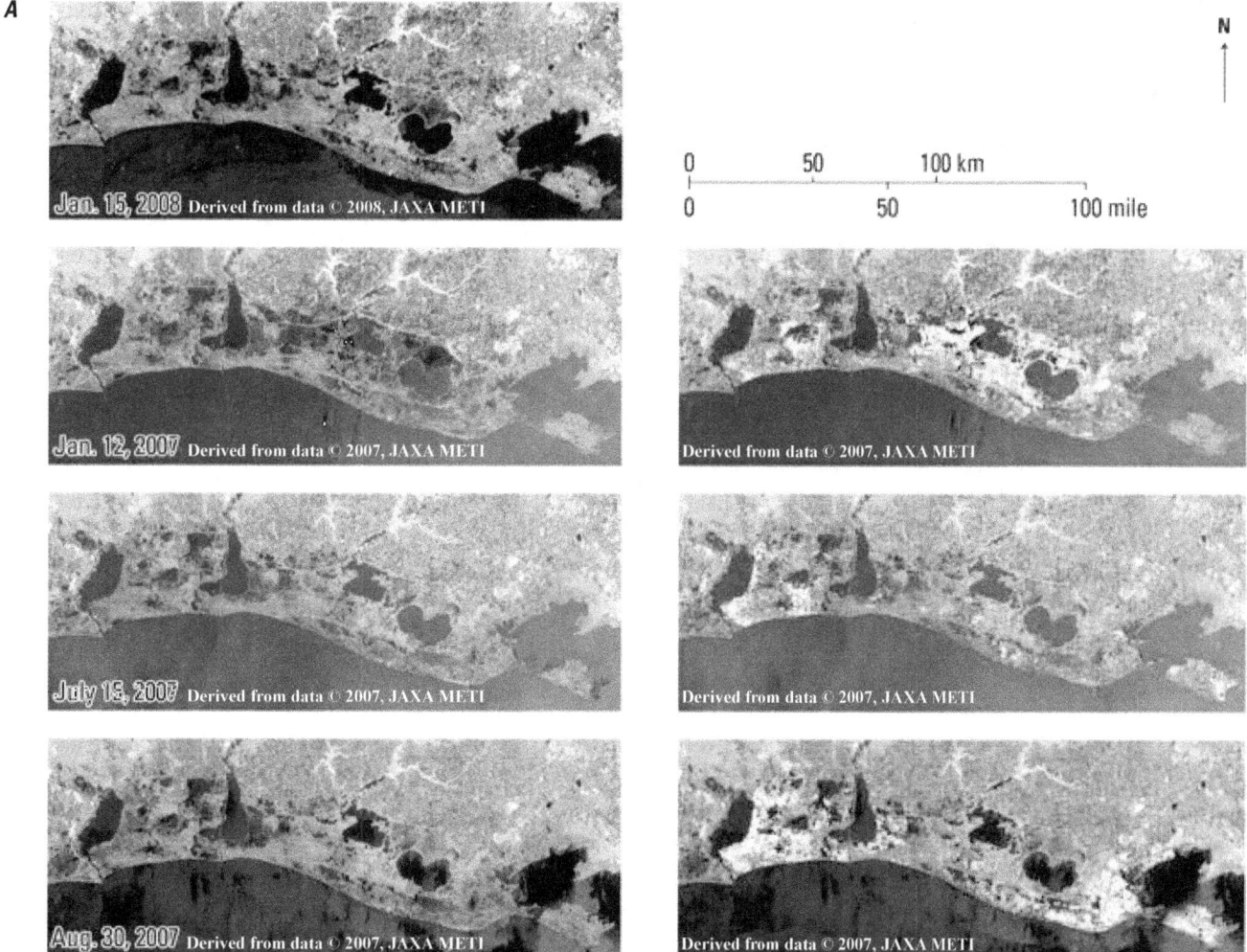

Figure 9.   Inundation maps created from Phased Array type L-band Synthetic Aperture Radar (PALSAR) scenes acquired by the Japanese Aerospace Exploration Agency's Advanced Land Observing Satellite. Inundation extents are expressed as a color overlay and were derived from interpretation of changes in decibels (σ_0) between the target and reference PALSAR scenes (PCI, 2007; Ramsey, Werle, and others, in press). PALSAR scenes on the left are dated according to scene acquisition; color-adjusted scenes (right panel) indicate detected areas of inundation. A, Results for the western coastal region. The reference PALSAR scene was acquired on January 15, 2008. B, Results for the eastern coastal region. The reference PALSAR scene was acquired on January 7, 2007.

A

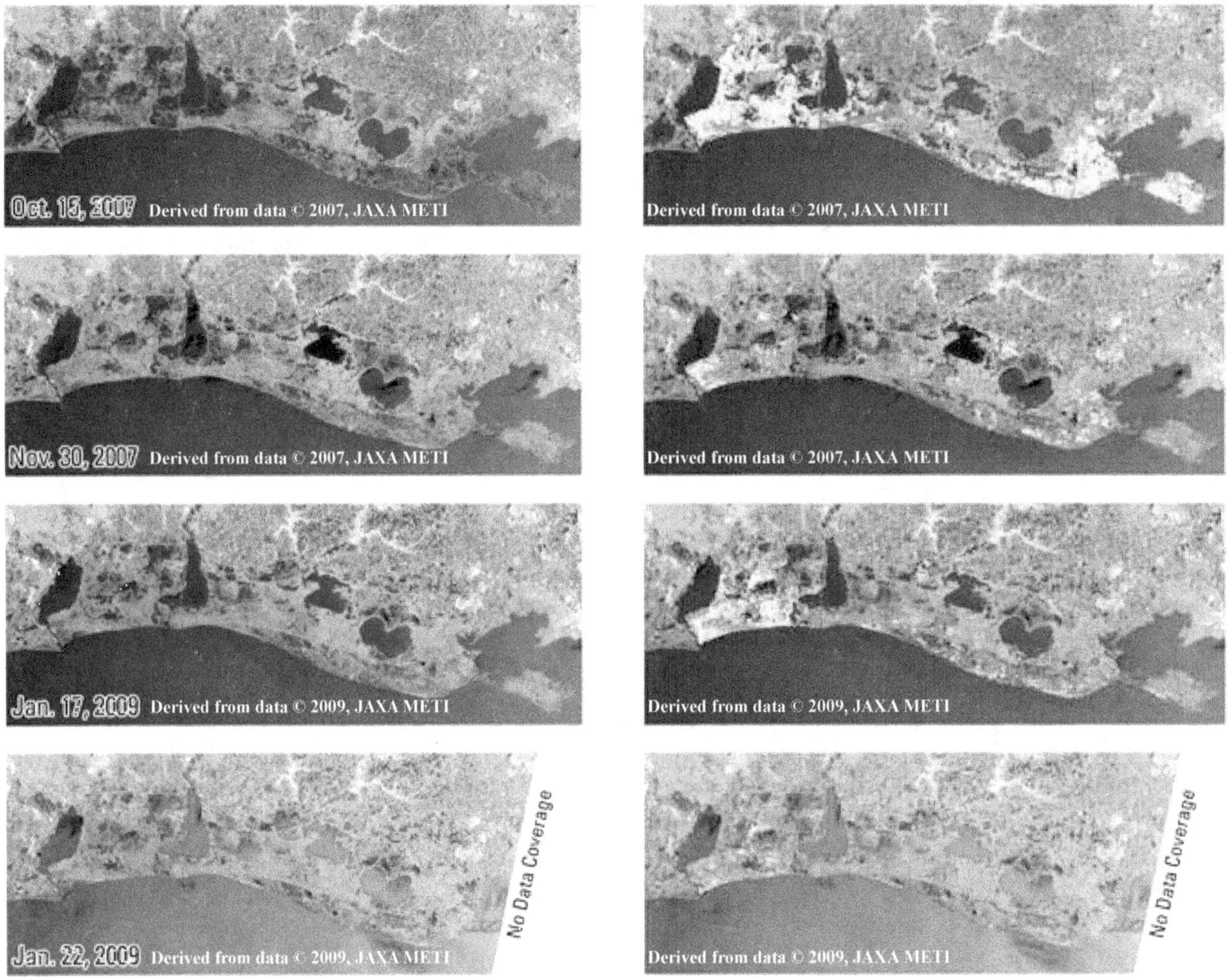

Figure 9.—Continued   Inundation maps created from Phased Array type L-band Synthetic Aperture Radar (PALSAR) scenes acquired by the Japanese Aerospace Exploration Agency's Advanced Land Observing Satellite. Inundation extents are expressed as a color overlay and were derived from interpretation of changes in decibels (σ_0) between the target and reference PALSAR scenes (PCI, 2007; Ramsey, Werle, and others, in press). PALSAR scenes on the left are dated according to scene acquisition; color-adjusted scenes (right panel) indicate detected areas of inundation. *A*, Results for the western coastal region. The reference PALSAR scene was acquired on January 15, 2008. *B*, Results for the eastern coastal region. The reference PALSAR scene was acquired on January 7, 2007.

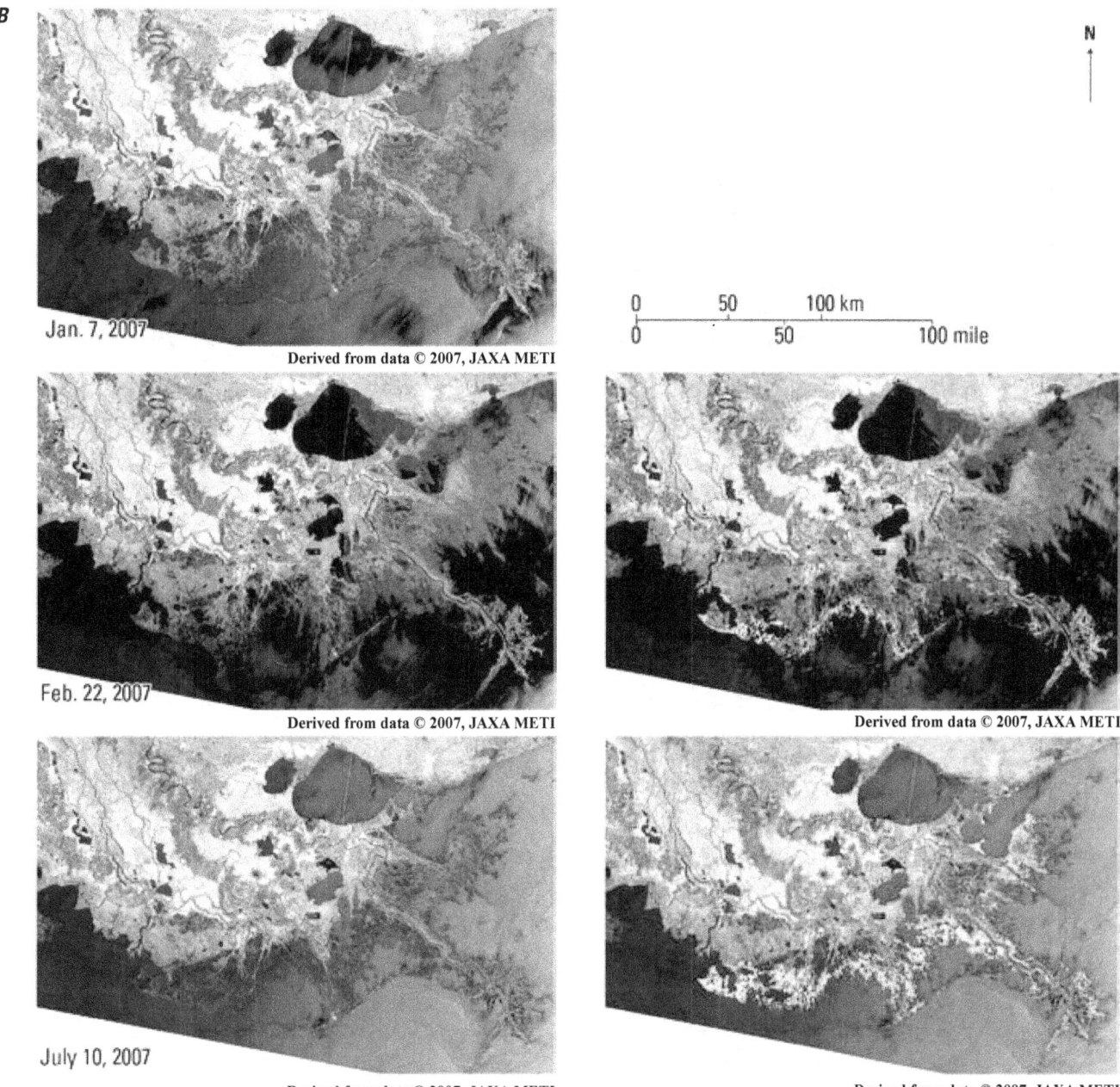

N

0   50   100 km

0   50   100 mile

B

Jan. 7, 2007

Derived from data © 2007, JAXA METI

Feb. 22, 2007

Derived from data © 2007, JAXA METI

Derived from data © 2007, JAXA METI

July 10, 2007

Derived from data © 2007, JAXA METI

Derived from data © 2007, JAXA METI

Figure 9.—Continued   Inundation maps created from Phased Array type L-band Synthetic Aperture Radar (PALSAR) scenes acquired by the Japanese Aerospace Exploration Agency's Advanced Land Observing Satellite. Inundation extents are expressed as a color overlay and were derived from interpretation of changes in decibels (σ_0) between the target and reference PALSAR scenes (PCI, 2007; Ramsey, Werle, and others, in press). PALSAR scenes on the left are dated according to scene acquisition; color-adjusted scenes (right panel) indicate detected areas of inundation. *A*, Results for the western coastal region. The reference PALSAR scene was acquired on January 15, 2008. *B*, Results for the eastern coastal region. The reference PALSAR scene was acquired on January 7, 2007.

B

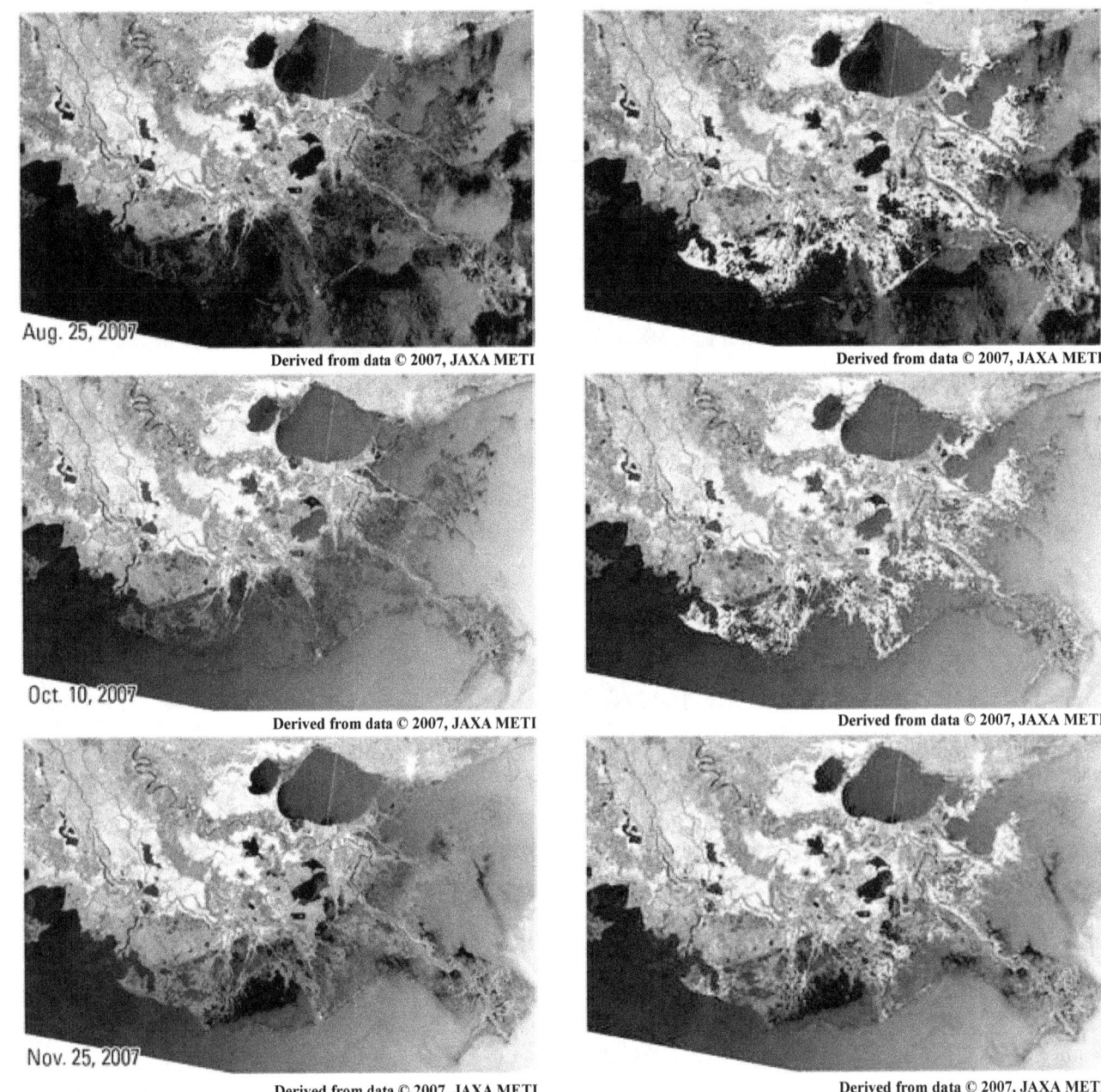

Aug. 25, 2007

Derived from data © 2007, JAXA METI

Derived from data © 2007, JAXA METI

Oct. 10, 2007

Derived from data © 2007, JAXA METI

Derived from data © 2007, JAXA METI

Nov. 25, 2007

Derived from data © 2007, JAXA METI

Derived from data © 2007, JAXA METI

Figure 9.—Continued Inundation maps created from Phased Array type L-band Synthetic Aperture Radar (PALSAR) scenes acquired by the Japanese Aerospace Exploration Agency's Advanced Land Observing Satellite. Inundation extents are expressed as a color overlay and were derived from interpretation of changes in decibels (σ_0) between the target and reference PALSAR scenes (PCI, 2007; Ramsey, Werle, and others, in press). PALSAR scenes on the left are dated according to scene acquisition; color-adjusted scenes (right panel) indicate detected areas of inundation. *A*, Results for the western coastal region. The reference PALSAR scene was acquired on January 15, 2008. *B*, Results for the eastern coastal region. The reference PALSAR scene was acquired on January 7, 2007.

B

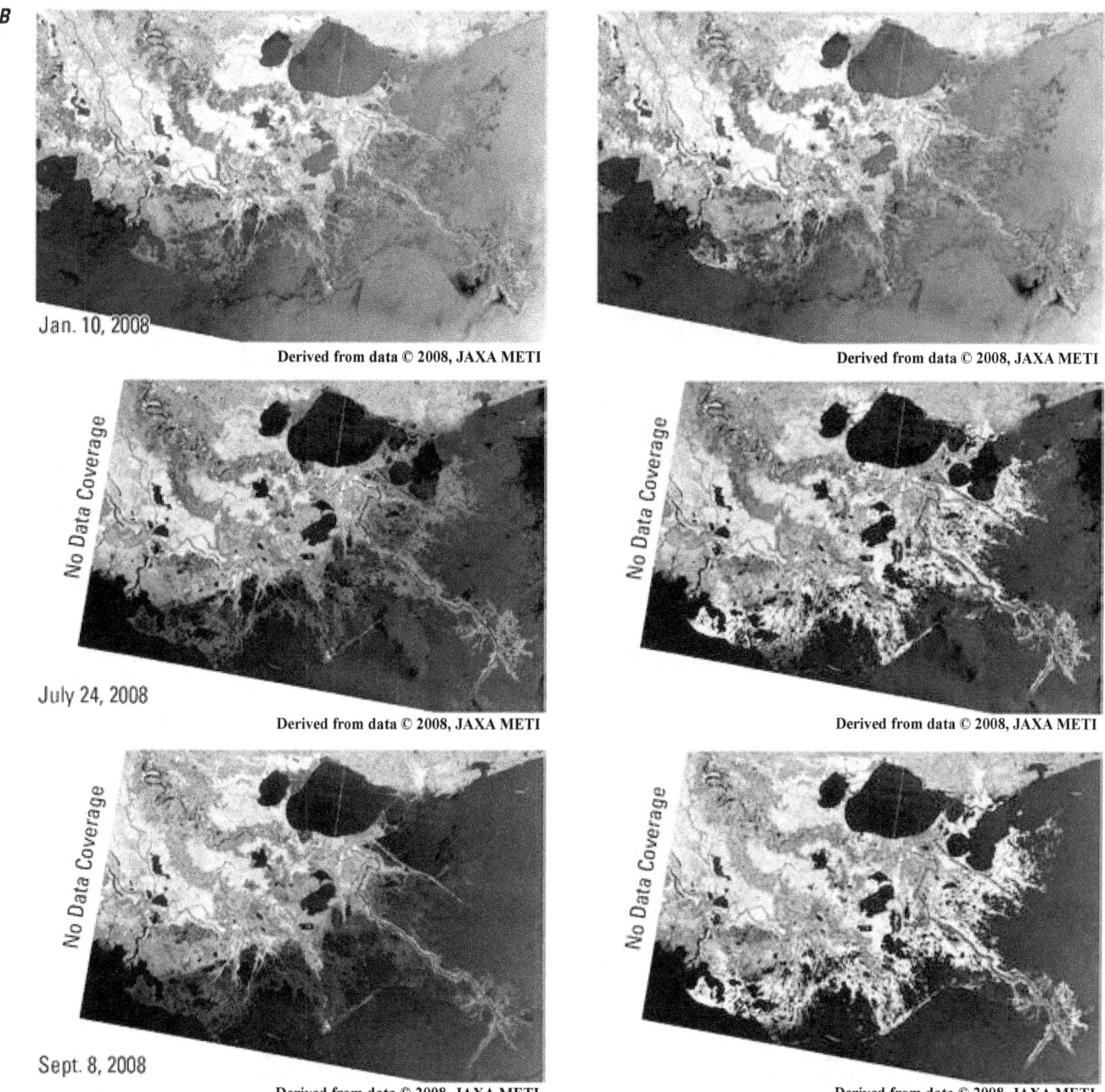

Jan. 10, 2008

Derived from data © 2008, JAXA METI

No Data Coverage

July 24, 2008

Derived from data © 2008, JAXA METI

No Data Coverage

Derived from data © 2008, JAXA METI

No Data Coverage

Sept. 8, 2008

Derived from data © 2008, JAXA METI

No Data Coverage

Derived from data © 2008, JAXA METI

Figure 9.—Continued   Inundation maps created from Phased Array type L-band Synthetic Aperture Radar (PALSAR) scenes acquired by the Japanese Aerospace Exploration Agency's Advanced Land Observing Satellite. Inundation extents are expressed as a color overlay and were derived from interpretation of changes in decibels (σ_0) between the target and reference PALSAR scenes (PCI, 2007; Ramsey, Werle, and others, in press). PALSAR scenes on the left are dated according to scene acquisition; color-adjusted scenes (right panel) indicate detected areas of inundation. *A*, Results for the western coastal region. The reference PALSAR scene was acquired on January 15, 2008. *B*, Results for the eastern coastal region. The reference PALSAR scene was acquired on January 7, 2007.

B

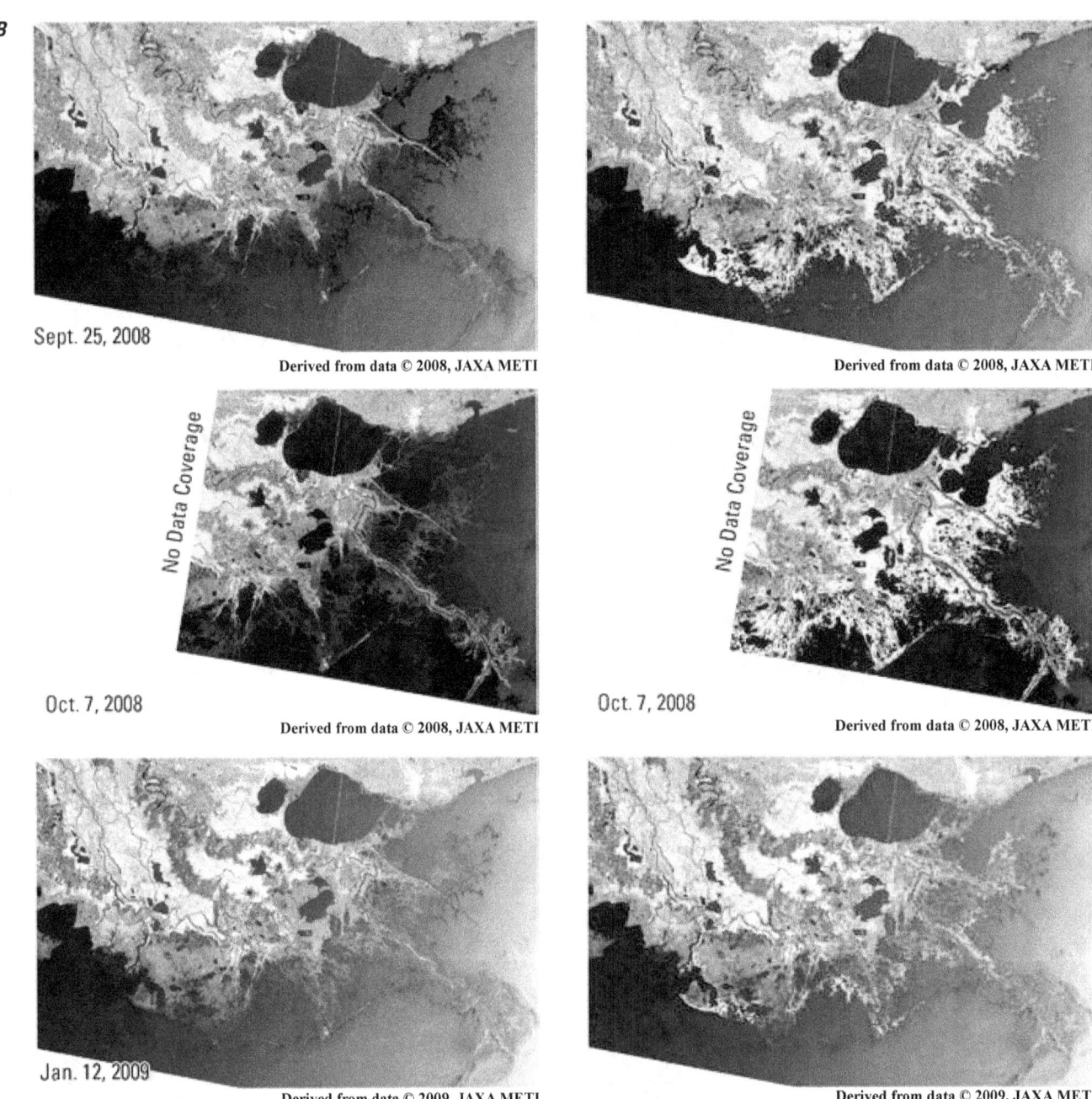

Sept. 25, 2008

Derived from data © 2008, JAXA METI

Derived from data © 2008, JAXA METI

Oct. 7, 2008

Derived from data © 2008, JAXA METI

Oct. 7, 2008

Derived from data © 2008, JAXA METI

Jan. 12, 2009

Derived from data © 2009, JAXA METI

Derived from data © 2009, JAXA METI

Figure 9.—Continued   Inundation maps created from Phased Array type L-band Synthetic Aperture Radar (PALSAR) scenes acquired by the Japanese Aerospace Exploration Agency's Advanced Land Observing Satellite. Inundation extents are expressed as a color overlay and were derived from interpretation of changes in decibels (σ_0) between the target and reference PALSAR scenes (PCI, 2007; Ramsey, Werle, and others, in press). PALSAR scenes on the left are dated according to scene acquisition; color-adjusted scenes (right panel) indicate detected areas of inundation. *A*, Results for the western coastal region. The reference PALSAR scene was acquired on January 15, 2008. *B*, Results for the eastern coastal region. The reference PALSAR scene was acquired on January 7, 2007.

B

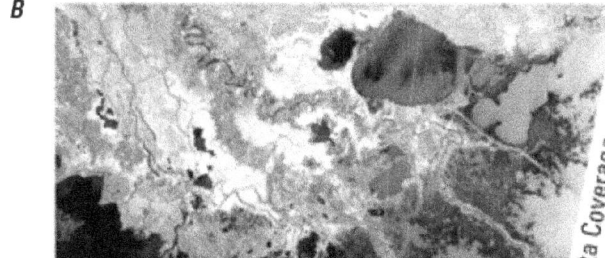

Sept. 16, 2009

Derived from data © 2009, JAXA METI

No Data Coverage

Derived from data © 2009, JAXA METI

Figure 9.—Continued   Inundation maps created from Phased Array type L-band Synthetic Aperture Radar (PALSAR) scenes acquired by the Japanese Aerospace Exploration Agency's Advanced Land Observing Satellite. Inundation extents are expressed as a color overlay and were derived from interpretation of changes in decibels (σ_0) between the target and reference PALSAR scenes (PCI, 2007; Ramsey, Werle, and others, in press). PALSAR scenes on the left are dated according to scene acquisition; color-adjusted scenes (right panel) indicate detected areas of inundation. *A*, Results for the western coastal region. The reference PALSAR scene was acquired on January 15, 2008. *B*, Results for the eastern coastal region. The reference PALSAR scene was acquired on January 7, 2007.

Table 10.   Results of inundation-change analysis for the western Louisiana coast compared with water-level measurements at inland hydrologic stations along the coast. PCI image processing software was used to identify changes between the reference- and target-Synthetic Aperture Radar (SAR) scenes that represented inundation on the target scene (PCI, 2007; Ramsey, Werle, and others, in press). Phased Array type L-band SAR (PALSAR) data were acquired by the Japanese Aerospace Exploration Agency's Advanced Land Observing Satellite. Inland water levels were measured against marsh-surface height.

[Water-level measurements are provided in meters. PALSAR; Phased Array type L-band Synthetic Aperture Radar; CRMS, Coastwide Reference Monitoring System; ID, identification; n.d., no data; PALSAR scenes used in the change-detection analysis exhibited horizontal transmit and receive polarization; CHDET, change-detection analysis]

| | PALSAR acquisition dates and inland water levels | | | | | | | |
| | 2008 | 2007 | | | | | 2009 | |
CRMS Station ID	**Jan. 15**	**Jan. 12**	**July 15**	**Aug. 30**	**Oct. 15**	**Nov. 30**	**Jan. 17**	**Jan. 22**
665	0.082	n.d.	n.d.	n.d.	n.d.	n.d.	0.149	0.134
682	-.189	n.d.	n.d.	n.d.	n.d.	-.009	-.101	-.140
588	n.d.	n.d.	n.d.	.107	.189	n.d.	n.d.	n.d.
599	-.101	-.030	n.d.	.055	.198	-.101	n.d.	n.d.
609	-.140	n.d.	n.d.	n.d.	n.d.	n.d.	-.125	-.143
576	n.d.	n.d.	n.d.	n.d.	n.d.	n.d.	-.119	-.189
508	n.d.	n.d.	n.d.	n.d.	n.d.	n.d.	-.268	-.268
2189	-.018	n.d.	n.d.	.085	.192	.012	.027	.000
680	.024	n.d.	n.d.	.058	.085	.055	n.d.	n.d.
553	.195	n.d.	.299	.274	.347	n.d.	.186	.143
623	n.d.	n.d.	n.d.	n.d.	n.d.	n.d.	n.d.	n.d.
1277	n.d.	n.d.	n.d.	n.d.	n.d.	n.d.	n.d.	n.d.

Water levels corresponding to acquisition of the PALSAR reference scene on January 15, 2008.

CHDET results were consistent with water levels measured at CRMS stations.

CHDET results were not consistent with water levels measured at CRMS stations.

Either PALSAR data or site-specific water-level measurements were not available on the given date.

Table 11.   Results of inundation-change analysis for the eastern Louisiana coast compared with water-level measurements at inland hydrologic stations along the Louisiana coast. PCI image processing software was used to identify changes between the reference- and target-Synthetic Aperture Radar (SAR) scenes that represented inundation on the target scene (PCI, 2007; Ramsey, Werle, and others, in press). Phased Array type L-band SAR data were acquired by the Japanese Aerospace Exploration Agency's Advanced Land Observing Satellite. Inland water levels were measured against marsh-surface height.

[Water-level measurements are provided in meters. PALSAR; Phased Array type L-band Synthetic Aperture Radar; CRMS, Coastwide Reference Monitoring System; ID, identification; n.d., no data; PALSAR scenes used in the change-detection analysis exhibited horizontal transmit and receive polarization; CHDET, change-detection analysis]

| CRMS station ID | PALSAR acquisition dates and inland water levels | | | | | | | | | | | | |
| | 2007 | 2007 | | | | | 2008 | | | | | 2009 | |
	Jan. 7	Feb. 22	July 10	Aug. 25	Oct. 10	Nov. 25	Jan. 10	July 24	Sept. 8	Sept. 25	Oct. 7	Jan. 12	Sept. 16
374	-0.250	-0.113	-0.021	0.152	0.104	-0.311	-0.317	0.006	0.091	0.235	0.012	n.d.	n.d.
311	-.137	-.030	.180	.283	.180	-.229	-.192	.140	.241	.351	.241	-.384	.375
338	-.168	-.034	.180	.311	.162	-.250	-.131	.113	.024	n.d.	n.d.	n.d.	.451
4218	n.d	n.d	n.d.	n.d.	n.d.	n.d.	n.d.	.088	.213	.296	.253	-.256	.363
261	n.d	n.d	.061	.162	.171	-.079	n.d.	.128	.250	.283	.296	-.238	.390
251	-.018	-.122	.171	.274	.152	-.113	-.049	.125	.140	.472	.280	n.d.	.466
3667	n.d	n.d	n.d.	n.d.	.207	.091	.006	n.d.	n.d.	.332	.381	-.140	.268
30	n.d	n.d	-.076	.131	.283	.290	.091	-.046	.351	.448	.466	-.003	.396
33	n.d	n.d	-.177	.058	.305	.122	.015	-.101	.341	.372	.329	-.149	.317
146	n.d	n.d	n.d.	n.d.	n.d.	.238	-.037	-.064	.317	.427	n.d.	n.d.	n.d.
136	-.290	-.402	-.128	.058	.034	.000	-.320	-.219	.213	.530	.158	n.d.	.226
4529	n.d	n.d	n.d.	.274	.168	-.247	-.155	.058	.195	.247	.113	-.463	.475
147	-.326	-.183	-.009	.256	.216	-.262	n.d.	-.162	n.d.	.433	.101	-.280	.436
4572	n.d	n.d	n.d.	n.d.	n.d.	.098	-.235	-.070	n.d.	.472	.311	-.287	.494

Water levels corresponding to acquisition of the PALSAR reference scene on January 7, 2008.

Change-detection results were consistent with water levels measured at CRMS stations.

Change-detection results were not consistent with water levels measured at CRMS stations.

Either PALSAR data or site-specific water-level measurements were not available on the given date.

A

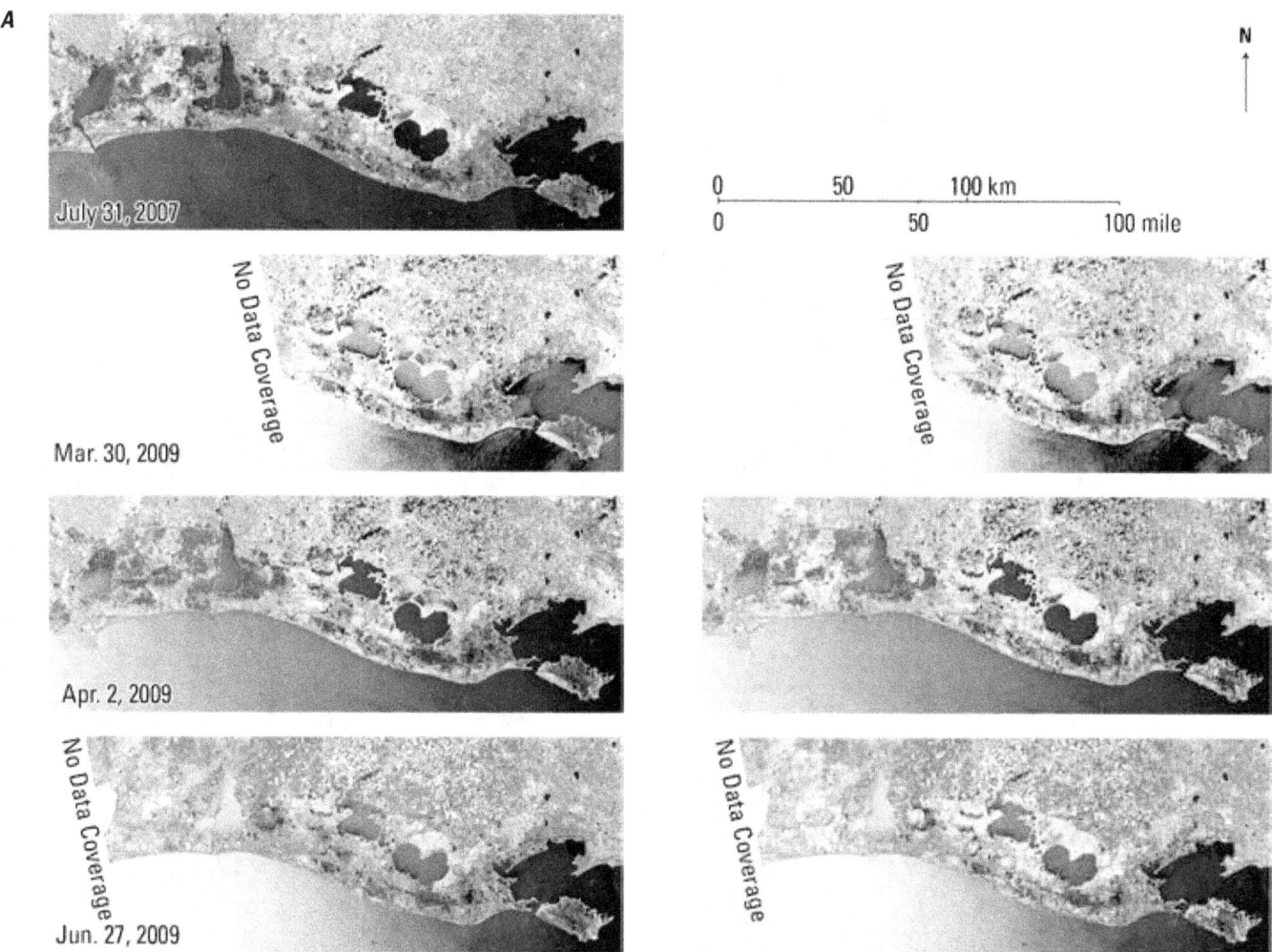

N
↑

Figure 10. Maps created from Advanced Synthetic Aperture Radar (ASAR) scenes exhibiting horizontal transmit and receive (HH) polarization that were acquired by the European Space Agency's Envisat. Inundation extents are expressed as a color overlay and were derived from interpretation of changes in decibels (σ_0) between the target and reference ASAR scenes (PCI, 2007; Ramsey, Werle, and others, in press). Images on the left are dated according to scene acquisition; color-adjusted scenes (right panel) indicate detected areas of inundation. *A*, Results for the western coastal region. The reference ASAR scene was acquired on July 31, 2007. *B*, Results for the eastern coastal region. The reference ASAR scene was acquired on March 30, 2009.

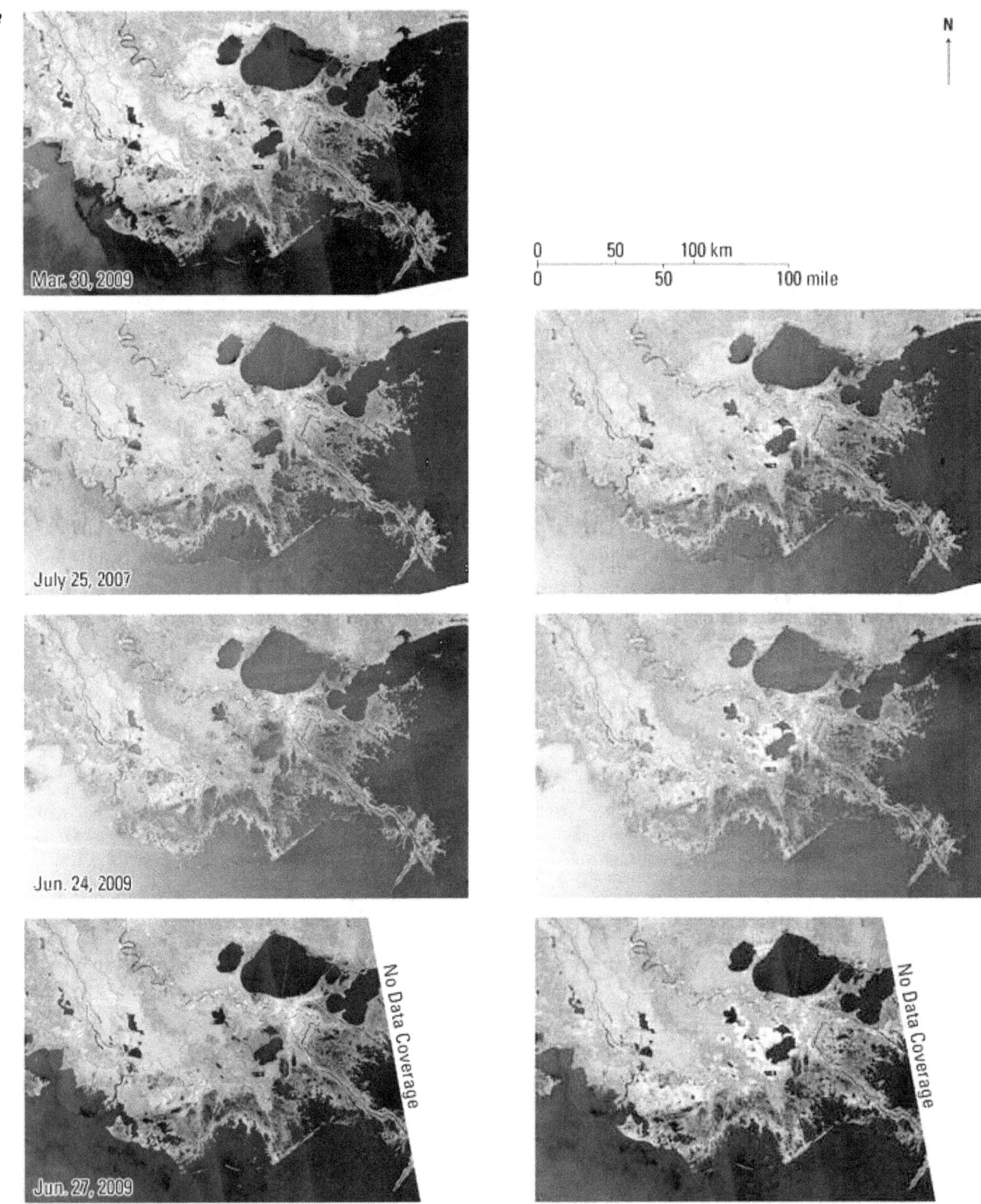

Figure 10.—Continued   Maps created from Advanced Synthetic Aperture Radar (ASAR) scenes exhibiting horizontal transmit and receive (HH) polarization that were acquired by the European Space Agency's Envisat. Inundation extents are expressed as a color overlay and were derived from interpretation of changes in decibels (σ_0) between the target and reference ASAR scenes (PCI, 2007; Ramsey, Werle, and others, in press). Images on the left are dated according to scene acquisition; color-adjusted scenes (right panel) indicate detected areas of inundation. *A*, Results for the western coastal region. The reference ASAR scene was acquired on July 31, 2007. *B*, Results for the eastern coastal region. The reference ASAR scene was acquired on March 30, 2009.

Table 12.   Results of inundation-change analysis for the western Louisiana coast compared with water-level measurements at inland hydrologic stations along the Louisiana coast. PCI image processing software was used to identify changes between the reference- and target-Synthetic Aperture Radar (SAR) horizontal transmit and receive polarization scenes that represented inundation on the target scene (PCI, 2007; Ramsey, Werle, and others, in press). Advanced SAR (ASAR) data were acquired by the European Space Agency's Envisat. Inland water levels were measured against marsh-surface height.

[Water-level measurements are provided in meters. ASAR; Advanced Synthetic Aperture Radar; CRMS, Coastwide Reference Monitoring System; ID, identification; n.d., no data; PALSAR scenes used in the change-detection analysis exhibited horizontal transmit and receive polarization; CHDET, change-detection analysis]

CRMS station ID	ASAR acquisition dates and inland water levels			
	2007	2009		
	July 31	Mar. 30	Apr. 2	June 27
665	n.d.	n.d.	0.162	-0.122
682	n.d.	-.006	-.012	-.247
588	.088	.131	.174	-.052
599	-.021	.055	.134	-.015
609	n.d.	.049	.091	.027
576	n.d.	.232	.201	-.055
508	n.d.	.137	.131	-.055
2189	.079	.061	.204	n.d.
680	.043	.046	.030	n.d.
553	.326	.250	.280	-.012
623	n.d.	.171	.183	-.076
1277	n.d.	.128	.119	-.113

Water levels corresponding to acquisition of the PALSAR reference scene on July 31, 2007.

CHDET results were consistent with water levels measured at CRMS stations.

CHDET results were not consistent with water levels measured at CRMS stations.

Either PALSAR data or site-specific water-level measurements were not available on the given date.

Table 13.   Results of inundation-change analysis for the eastern Louisiana coast compared with water-level measurements at inland hydrologic stations along the Louisiana coast. PCI image processing software was used to identify changes between the reference- and target-Synthetic Aperture Radar (SAR) horizontal transmit and receive polarization scenes that represented inundation on the target scene (PCI, 2007; Ramsey, Werle, and others, in press). Advanced SAR (ASAR) data were acquired by the European Space Agency's Envisat. Inland water levels were measured against marsh-surface height.

[Water-level measurements are provided in meters. ASAR; Advanced Synthetic Aperture Radar; CRMS, Coastwide Reference Monitoring System; ID, identification; n.d., no data; PALSAR scenes used in the change-detection analysis exhibited horizontal transmit and receive polarization; CHDET, change-detection analysis]

CRMS station ID	ASAR acquisition dates and inland water levels			
	2009	2007	2009	
	Mar. 30	July 25	June 24	June 27
374	n.d.	-0.079	n.d.	n.d.
311	-.198	-.052	-.195	-.034
338	-.287	-.027	-.32	-.082
4218	.006	n.d.	-.094	.04
261	.064	-.116	.003	.131
251	-.091	-.07	-.094	.098
3667	.168	n.d.	-.25	-.165
30	.125	.052	-.128	.101
33	.259	.009	-.259	-.067
146	-.061	n.d.	n.d.	n.d.
136	-.134	-.396	-.445	-.226
4529	-.274	n.d.	-.235	0
147	-.344	-.192	n.d.	n.d.
4572	-.18	n.d.	-.329	-.04

Water levels corresponding to acquisition of the PALSAR reference scene on March 30, 2009.

CHDET results were consistent with water levels measured at CRMS stations.

CHDET results were not consistent with water levels measured at CRMS stations.

Either PALSAR data or site-specific water-level measurements were not available on the given date.

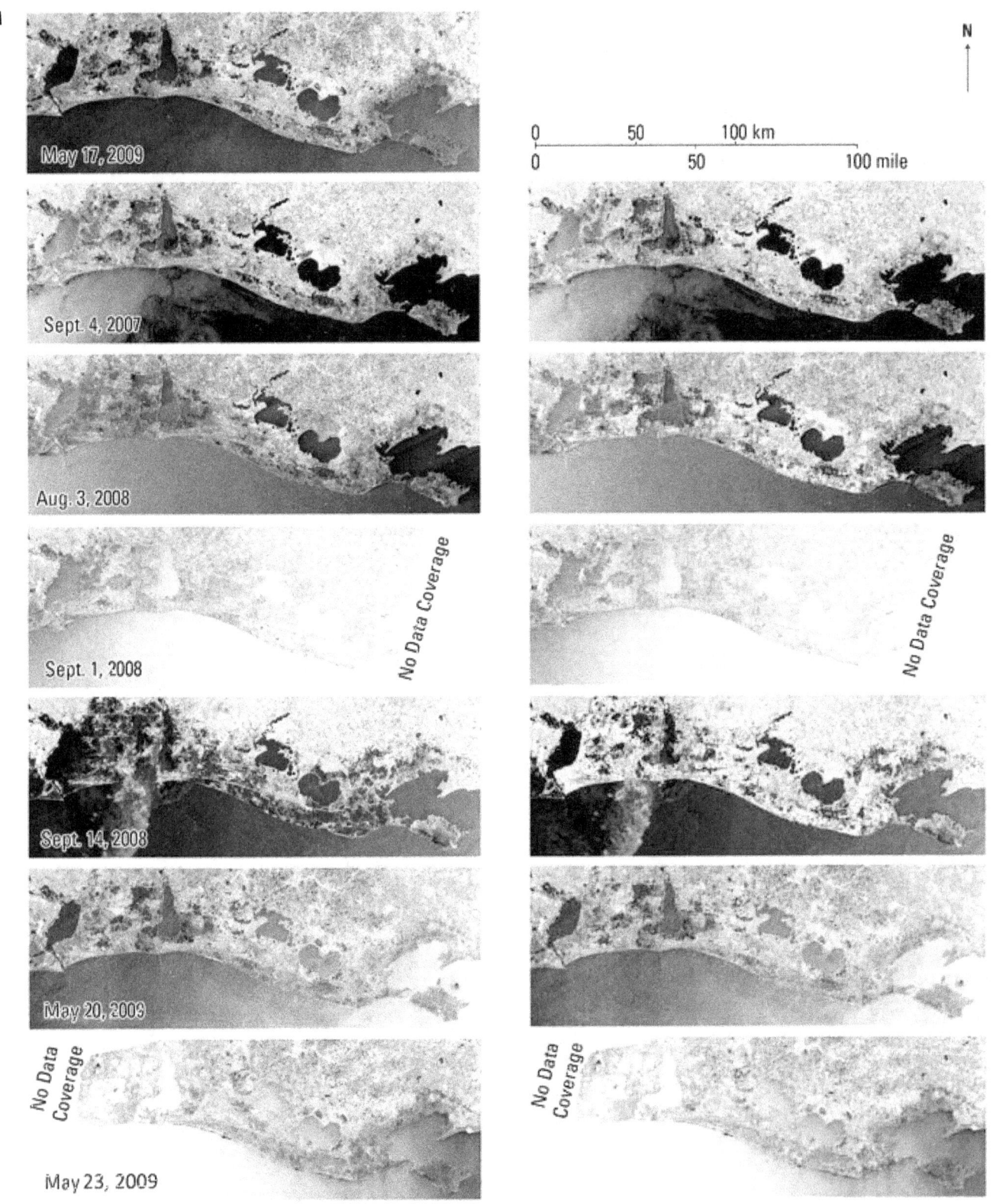

Figure 11. Inundation maps created from Advanced Synthetic Aperture Radar (ASAR) scenes exhibiting vertical transmit and receive (VV) polarization that were acquired by the European Space Agency's Envisat. Inundation extents are expressed as a color overlay and were derived from interpretation of changes in decibels (σ_0) between the target and reference ASAR scenes (PCI, 2007; Ramsey, Werle, and others, in press). Images in the left are dated according to scene acquisition; color-adjusted images (right panel) indicate detected areas of inundation. *A*, Results for the western coastal region. The reference ASAR scene was acquired on May 17, 2009. *B*, Results for the eastern coastal region. The reference ASAR scene was acquired on July 28, 2008.

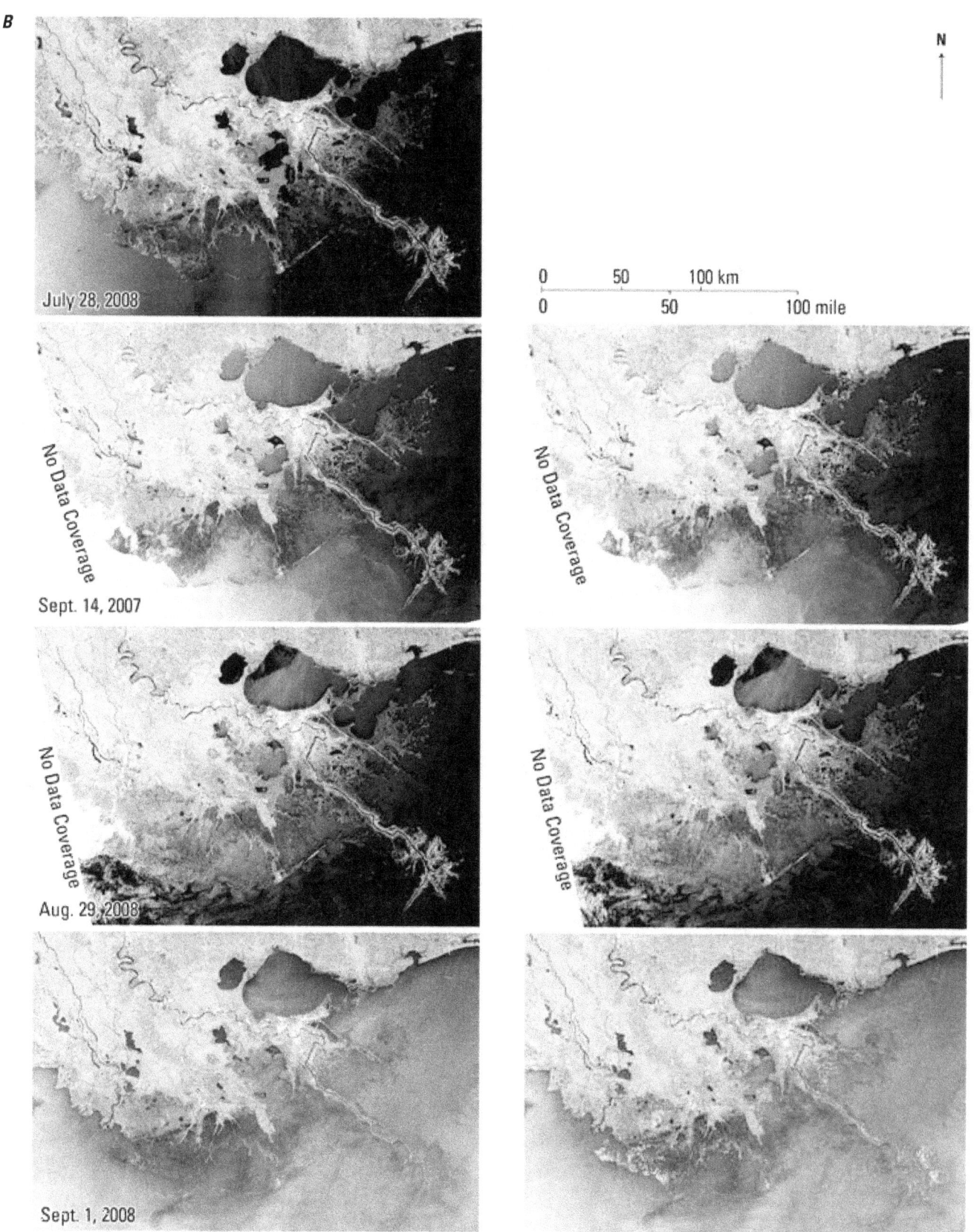

Figure 11.—Continued   Inundation maps created from Advanced Synthetic Aperture Radar (ASAR) scenes exhibiting vertical transmit and receive (VV) polarization that were acquired by the European Space Agency's Envisat. Inundation extents are expressed as a color overlay and were derived from interpretation of changes in decibels (σ_0) between the target and reference ASAR scenes (PCI, 2007; Ramsey, Werle, and others, in press). Images in the left are dated according to scene acquisition; color-adjusted images (right panel) indicate detected areas of inundation. *A*, Results for the western coastal region. The reference ASAR scene was acquired on May 17, 2009. *B*, Results for the eastern coastal region. The reference ASAR scene was acquired on July 28, 2008.

B

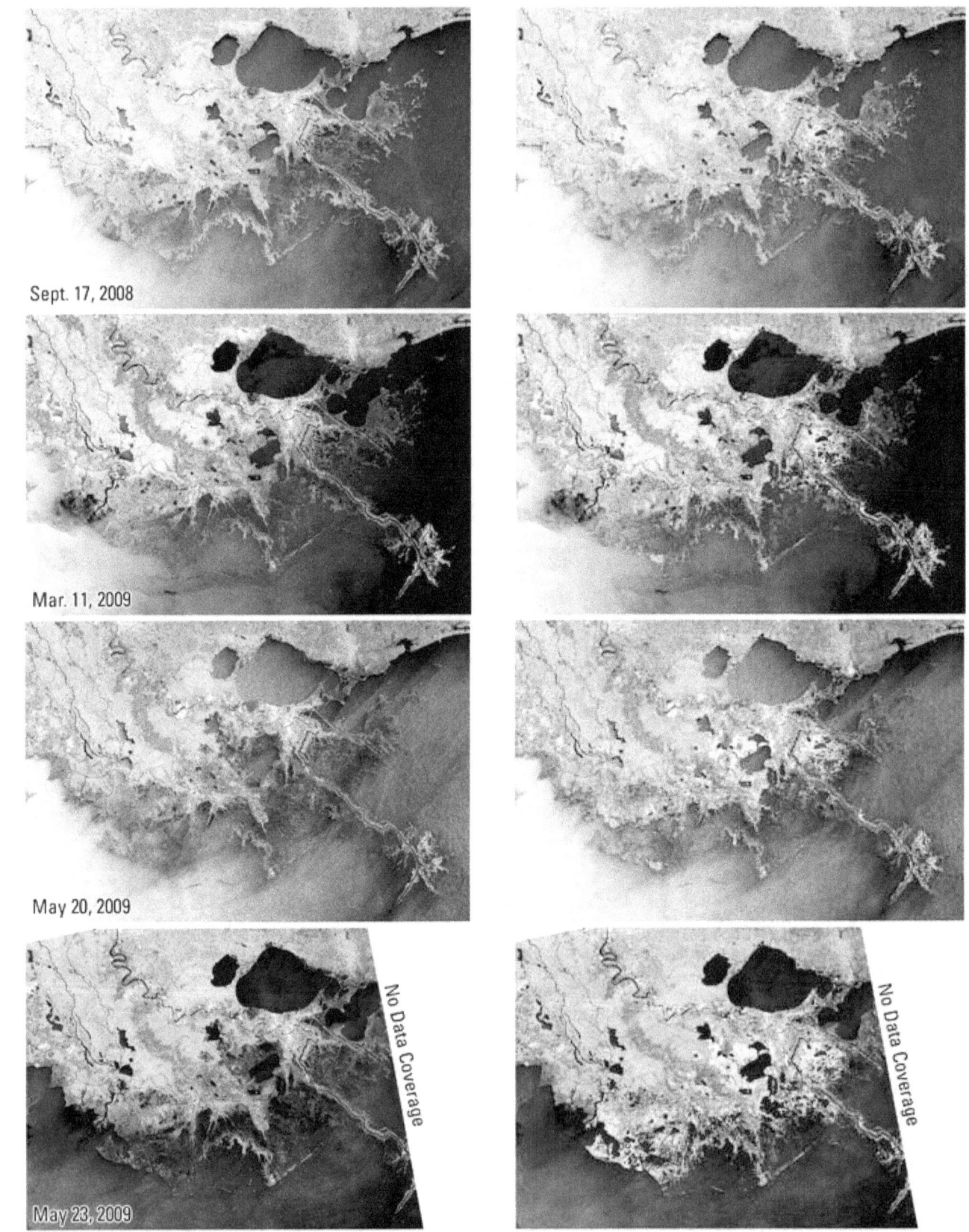

Figure 11.—Continued   Inundation maps created from Advanced Synthetic Aperture Radar (ASAR) scenes exhibiting vertical transmit and receive (VV) polarization that were acquired by the European Space Agency's Envisat. Inundation extents are expressed as a color overlay and were derived from interpretation of changes in decibels (σ_0) between the target and reference ASAR scenes (PCI, 2007; Ramsey, Werle, and others, in press). Images in the left are dated according to scene acquisition; color-adjusted images (right panel) indicate detected areas of inundation. *A*, Results for the western coastal region. The reference ASAR scene was acquired on May 17, 2009. *B*, Results for the eastern coastal region. The reference ASAR scene was acquired on July 28, 2008.

B

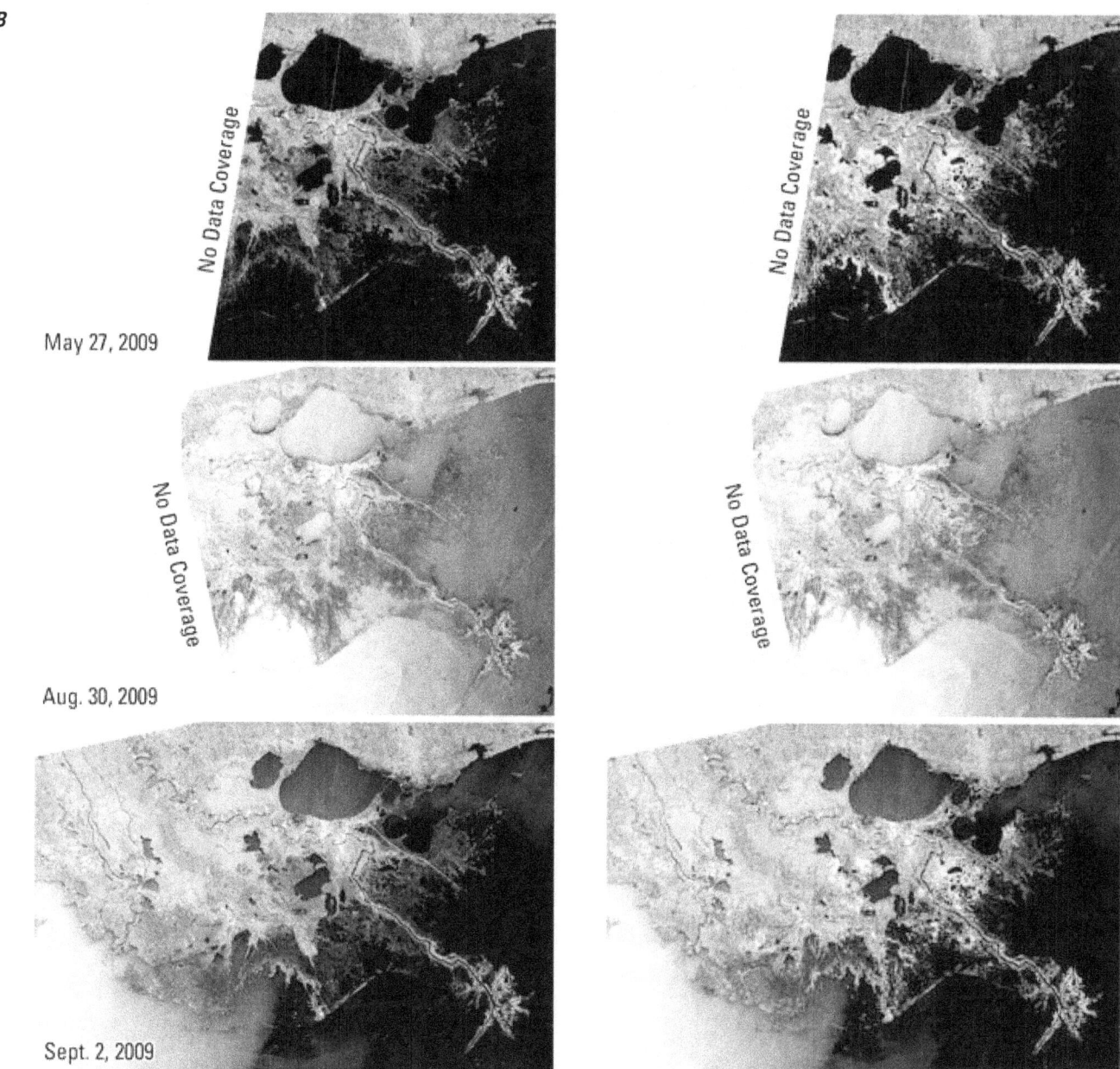

May 27, 2009

Aug. 30, 2009

Sept. 2, 2009

Figure 11.—Continued   Inundation maps created from Advanced Synthetic Aperture Radar (ASAR) scenes exhibiting vertical transmit and receive (VV) polarization that were acquired by the European Space Agency's Envisat. Inundation extents are expressed as a color overlay and were derived from interpretation of changes in decibels (σ_0) between the target and reference ASAR scenes (PCI, 2007; Ramsey, Werle, and others, in press). Images in the left are dated according to scene acquisition; color-adjusted images (right panel) indicate detected areas of inundation. *A*, Results for the western coastal region. The reference ASAR scene was acquired on May 17, 2009. *B*, Results for the eastern coastal region. The reference ASAR scene was acquired on July 28, 2008.

Table 14.   Results of inundation-change analysis for the western Louisiana coast compared with water-level measurements at inland hydrologic stations along the Louisiana coast. PCI image processing software was used to identify changes between the reference- and target-Synthetic Aperture Radar (SAR) vertical transmit and receive polarization scenes that represented inundation on the target scene (PCI, 2007; Ramsey, Werle, and others, in press). Advanced SAR (ASAR) data were acquired by the European Space Agency's Envisat. Inland water levels were measured against marsh-surface height.

[Water-level measurements are provided in meters. ASAR; Advanced Synthetic Aperture Radar; CRMS, Coastwide Reference Monitoring System; ID, identification; n.d., no data; ASAR scenes used in the change-detection analysis exhibited vertical transmit and receive polarization; CHDET, change-detection analysis]

CRMS station ID	ASAR acquisition dates and inland water levels						
	2009	2007	2008			2009	
	May 17	Sept. 4	Aug. 3	Sept. 1	Sept. 14	May 20	May 23
665	0.296	n.d.	0.158	0.162	1.548	0.302	0.113
682	-.064	n.d.	-.140	.034	1.655	-.067	-.061
588	.128	.128	.040	-.034	1.180	.091	.107
599	.009	-.024	n.d.	.015	.884	.101	.146
609	-.03	n.d.	-.040	-.113	1.152	.018	.049
576	.101	n.d.	.052	.070	1.189	.064	.113
508	-.131	n.d.	-.064	-.195	1.228	-.006	.037
2189	.085	.040	.037	-.052	n.d.	.055	.104
680	-.043	.027	n.d.	.021	1.679	-.061	-.061
553	.354	.302	.271	.280	1.628	.317	.287
623	.064	n.d.	.000	-.223	1.097	.024	.076
1277	.1463	n.d.	-.354	-.213	.165	.104	.098

Water levels corresponding to acquisition of the PALSAR reference scene on May 17, 2009.

CHDET results were consistent with water levels measured at CRMS stations.

CHDET results were not consistent with water levels measured at CRMS stations.

Either PALSAR data or site-specific water-level measurements were not available on the given date.

A storm cell created high backscatter around CRMS0682 and CRMS0680. The flood peak was delayed at CRMS1277.

The highest number of inundation maps was created from ASAR VV scenes covering the eastern coastal region (fig. 11*B*). For this region, the overall correspondence rate of ASAR-based inundation maps with coastal and inland water levels was 61 percent, which included scenes acquired on August 29 and March 11, 2008, when water levels below marsh-surface dominated. The overall correspondence rate also included scenes acquired on May 23 and 27, 2009, when relatively high water levels above the marsh-surface were recorded (fig. 11*B*, table 15).Conversely, scenes in the eastern region that were acquired on September 1 and 17, 2009, when there were moderately high surface-water levels, yielded low correspondence with coastal and inland water-level data. On September 1 and May 20, 2009, marsh over-topping accompanied by wind or rain roughening of the surface water increased SAR backscatter, thereby reducing the effectiveness SAR-based inundation mapping in many near coastal locations (fig.11*B*) (Ramsey and others, 1994, 2009; Ramsey, Werle, and others, in press).

Although these known environmental conditions may have explained the low correspondence rates of the September 1 and May 20, 2009, scenes, the wind roughening of the water surfaces was not indicated as a factor in the low correspondence rates of the September 17, 2008, scene, which was also associated with relatively high water levels. Alternatively, low correspondence of the September 17, 2008, scene was likely due to a mixture of residual ponding of surface water and high water content in sediment following Hurricane Ike-induced coastal inundations that occurred in the east from about September 13 to 14, 2008. The ponded water would tend to decrease backscatter while the high water content in sediment at below saturation would tend to enhance backscatter (Ramsey and others, 1999). As in wind roughening, surface-water ponding would tend to lower the detection-based inundation mapping performance. The lower correspondences of the May 11and (in part) the May 23, 2009, scenes were mostly associated with near-surface water levels.

Table 15. Results of inundation-change analysis for the eastern Louisiana coast compared with water-level measurements at inland hydrologic stations along the Louisiana coast. PCI image processing software was used to identify changes between the reference- and target-Synthetic Aperture Radar (SAR) vertical transmit and receive polarization scenes that represented inundation on the target scene (PCI, 2007; Ramsey, Werle, and others, in press Advanced SAR (ASAR) data were acquired by the European Space Agency's Envisat. Inland water levels were measured against marsh-surface height.

[Water-level measurements are provided in meters. ASAR; Advanced Synthetic Aperture Radar; CRMS, Coastwide Reference Monitoring System; ID, identification; n.d., no data; ASAR scenes used in the change-detection analysis exhibited vertical transmit and receive polarization; CHDET, change-detection results]

| Station ID | ASAR acquisition dates and inland water levels | | | | | | | | | | |
| | 2008 | 2007 | 2008 | | | 2009 | | | | | |
	July 28	Sept. 14	Aug. 29	Sept. 1	Sept. 17	Mar. 11	May 20	May 23	May 27	Aug. 30	Sept. 2
374	-0.101	-0.049	-0.265	-0.006	0.137	-0.061	0.043	-0.052	0.299	n.d.	n.d.
311	-.055	.146	-.207	.073	.210	.012	.088	.006	.344	-.021	-.140
338	-.104	.189	-.216	-.064	.296	.070	.268	.055	.338	n.d.	n.d.
4218	-.14	n.d.	-.110	-.021	.207	.034	-.024	.094	.146	-.006	-.070
261	-.076	.195	-.073	-.018	.250	.030	-.024	.128	.183	.055	-.015
251	-.128	.189	-.140	-.018	.570	.067	.003	.064	.232	.049	-.079
3667	NA	n.d.	n.d.	n.d.	.229	-.076	.259	.418	.101	.076	.012
30	-.204	.101	-.027	.204	.351	-.021	.347	.500	.076	.091	.043
33	-.143	.104	-.091	.076	.418	-.070	.290	.399	.177	.088	.027
146	-.277	n.d.	-.119	.277	.168	-.119	.192	.405	n.d.	n.d.	n.d.
136	-.564	-.277	-.411	.454	.283	-.192	.494	.539	.024	-.354	-.265
4529	-.11	.216	-.210	-.198	.183	.037	-.034	-.061	.326	.091	-.094
147	-.332	-.079	-.360	.701	.131	-.094	.091	.180	.094	n.d.	n.d.
4572	-.305	n.d.	-.351	.375	.241	-.070	.146	.216	.134	-.192	-.140

Water levels corresponding to acquisition of the PALSAR reference scene on July 28, 2008.

CHDET results were consistent with water levels measured at CRMS stations.

CHDET results were not consistent with water levels measured at CRMS stations.

Either PALSAR data or site-specific water-level measurements were not available on the given date.

Influence of Reference-Scene Selection on ASAR-Based Mapping Performance

To fully review the performance of ASAR-based mapping of inundation, it was desirable to demonstrate how dependent the performance was on ASAR reference-scene selection. To provide this demonstration, we mapped the inundation extent on an ASAR scene (with VV polarization) acquired on September 17, 2008—three to four days after Hurricane Ike surge flooding and about 14 days after Hurricane Gustav flooding in the east (Ramsey, Werle, and others, in press). For comparison, we used two different ASAR reference scenes to calculate the inundation extent. The first reference scene, acquired on March 11, 2009, was chosen solely based on coastal water levels. The second reference scene, acquired on July 28, 2008, was selected based on a combination of coastal and inland water levels. The resultant inundation distributions calculated for September 17, 2007, derived from the two different reference scenes highly diverged (fig. 12). The July 28 reference scene yielded a 43 percent correspondence between ASAR-based inundation and measured water-levels, which was a significant improvement over the 21 percent correspondence rate derived from the March 11, 2009, reference scene. The improved correspondence of inundation mapping based on the July 28, 2008, reference scene demonstrated a high degree of sensitivity exhibited by the ASAR-based inundation mapping that was not exhibited by the PALSAR-based inundation mapping.

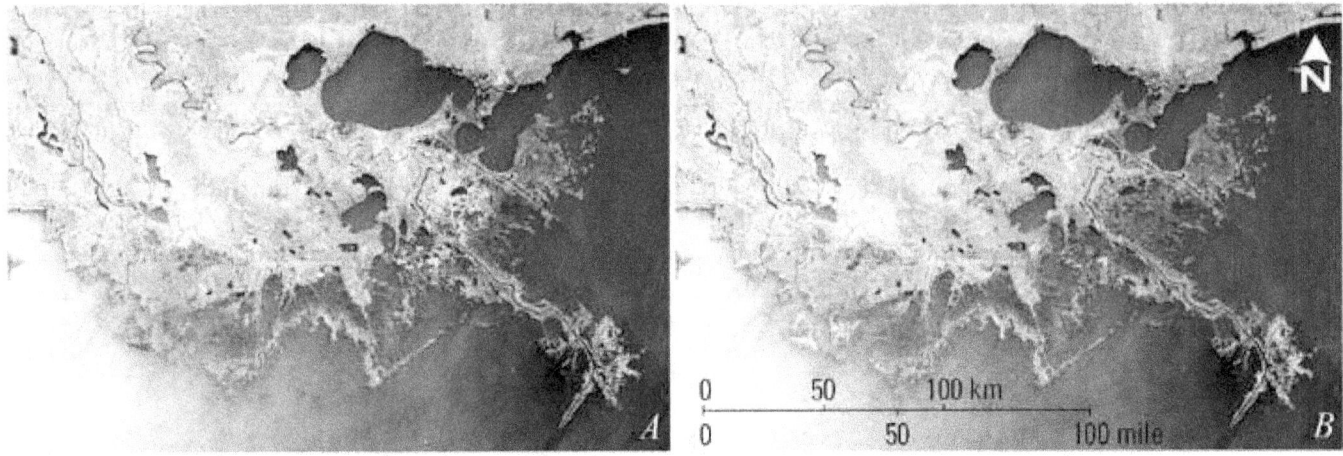

Figure 12. Inundation mapping results derived by using an Advanced Synthetic Aperture Radar (ASAR) target scene acquired on September 17, 2008, by the European Space Agency's Envisat. A comparison of results derived from using two different ASAR reference scenes is presented. *A*, Target scene paired with reference scene acquired July 28, 2008. *B*, Target scene paired with reference scene acquired March 11, 2009.

Discussion

SAR-based mapping of marsh inundation was compared to inland water-level records created when SAR scenes were acquired. Mapping success was determined by levels of correspondence between map and inland water-level records. Consistently higher mapping accuracies were obtained by using PALSAR (L-band) versus ASAR (C-band) data. Results for ASAR-based mapping also concluded that there were higher rates of correspondence when water levels were either much higher or much lower than the marsh-surface height. Additional comparisons were used to help explain variations in correspondence rates, particularly when using ASAR data.

Complications of ASAR-Based Inundation Mapping

Complications in the inundation mapping with the HH- and VV-polarized ASAR data stemmed to some extent from a lack of high-quality ASAR reference scenes. This paucity resulted from the abnormally high sea states in 2007 and 2008 that restricted the availability of ASAR reference scenes that completely fit the preferred criteria for reference selection. For the same reason, selection of appropriate reference scenes was also problematic in the PALSAR inundation mapping; however, high inconsistencies in ASAR scene collection

geometries seemed to intensify these problems and further hinder conformance between the ASAR reference and target scenes; collection parameters of all PALSAR scenes were highly similar from scene to scene.

Variability in collection geometries and coverage extents might not directly cause substantial problems in marsh inundation mapping but could more likely affect mapping performance through associated changes in the local incident angle. Although the local incident angle is not functionally related to coverage or look direction, particularly in flat terrains, in the coastal region studied, the higher the differences in coverage and look direction between scenes, the more dramatic the change in local incident angle at equivalent locations on the scenes. Differences in the local incident angle (as referenced to a set ground location) from scene to scene led to differences in SAR backscatter that were not compensated by calibration. Added to this causal variability in local incident angle, ASAR scenes exhibited higher sensitivity to changes in look angle from the near to far range than exhibited in the PALSAR scenes. This added sensitivity to progressive changes in look angle compounds complexities related to inconsistencies in the local incident angle and indirectly changes the relationship between the tested threshold value and the commission and omission errors throughout the inundation maps. Those differences in SAR backscatter due to the variability in the local incidence angle and progressive backscatter increases related to look angle would not represent differences in the presence or absence of inundation at that location. Because ASAR-based inundation mapping relied on scene-to-scene change detection, any anomalous, non-inundation-related changes confused the change-detection interpretation.

In effect, these erratic changes in backscatter unrelated to changes in inundation diminished the ASAR-based inundation mapping performance in ways that were undeterminable in this study. The consistent choice of reference scenes and deliberate identification of change-detection thresholds did reduce these types of change-detection misclassifications. In the case of ASAR, however, the high variety of compounding influences could not be fully compensated, thus resulting in lowered ASAR-based inundation mapping performance compared to PALSAR-based inundation mapping that used scenes with near consistency in collection geometries.

Visual Comparisons of SAR-based Inundation Maps

Although there were no coincident collections of PALSAR and ASAR scenes for use in this study, several useful observations can be made by using the current study results. First, PALSAR coverage in the eastern and western coastal regions included a majority of scenes indicating extensive and spatially contiguous areas of inundation versus scenes indicating scattered areas of inundation (figs. 9A,B). In contrast, most ASAR scenes covering the eastern and western coastal regions (with either HH or VV polarization) indicated limited and scattered areas of inundation (figs. 10A,B and 11A,B). The possibility exists that the PALSAR scenes were collected at times of more spatially extensive inundation compared to the times when ASAR scenes were collected; however, comparisons of SAR-based mapping and inland water-level records indicated that correspondences were high when using PALSAR-based maps and low when using ASAR-based maps when water levels were near the surface (tables 10–15). Visually, the PALSAR-based inundation maps exhibited more often contiguous inundation extents than ASAR-based inundation maps and PALSAR-based inundations more often corresponded with inland recordings than did ASAR-based inundations.

Validating SAR-based Inundation Maps with Inland Water-Level Data

Water-level data recorded at inland hydrologic stations were useful in elucidating the variable performance of SAR-based inundation mapping. Modeling and field studies of

Gulf of Mexico marshes have demonstrated that SAR (HH or VV polarization) backscatter decreases with increasing flood depth. Results of those studies have also confirmed that SAR backscatter can increase with increasing marsh biomass when the marsh is flooded, and backscatter can decrease with increasing biomass when marsh is not flooded. The decrease in backscatter when marsh is not flooded may be linked to the loss of enhanced backscatter associated with moist soils. These relationships between flooding and marsh biomass and backscatter are expected to be enhanced when using (L-band) PALSAR versus(C-band) ASAR systems because L-band has a higher potential for marsh penetration (Ramsey, 1998, 2005).

In order to add water-level data to the SAR-based inundation analyses, measurements recorded at inland hydrologic stations were depicted in separate graphics for each PALSAR and ASAR inundation map (figs. 13, 14, and 15).For 17 of the 19 PALSAR-based inundation maps covering locations where more than one or two data points for water levels existed, correspondence rates ranged 67–100 percent (figs. 13A, B). In one of the two cases where PALSAR results were lower than 85 percent (fig. 13B; scene from July 10, 2007), the correspondence was possibly lowered by contamination of the PALSAR pixel by nonmarsh land covers. In the second of these cases (fig. 9A,B), surface roughness of the surrounding inundated marshes seemed to lower mapping performance (Ramsey and others, 2009; Ramsey and others, 2011; Ramsey, Werle, and others, in press).Overall, inundation mapping by using PALSAR scenes with HH polarization performed exceedingly well. In nonflooded conditions, and at times of dominantly shallow or higher marsh flooding, the PALSAR-based inundation mapping corresponded with inland water-level recordings at rates exceeding 83 percent.

In contrast to PALSAR-based inundation mapping, ASAR-based mapping (using scenes with HH or VV polarization) did not perform as well. Most often, correspondence between ASAR-based inundation maps and inland water-level recordings was at rates around 60 percent (figs. 14 and 15). At times, correspondence rates dropped much lower (fig. 15B; scenes from Sept. 17, 2008, and Sept. 1,2009). In contrast, at a few times when water levels were ubiquitously below the ground surface (figs. 14B and 15B; scenes from July 25, 2007; June 24, 2009; and August 29, 2008) or nearly 1 m or more above marsh-surface height (fig. 15A; scene from Sept. 14, 2008), correspondence rates increased to higher than 76 percent.

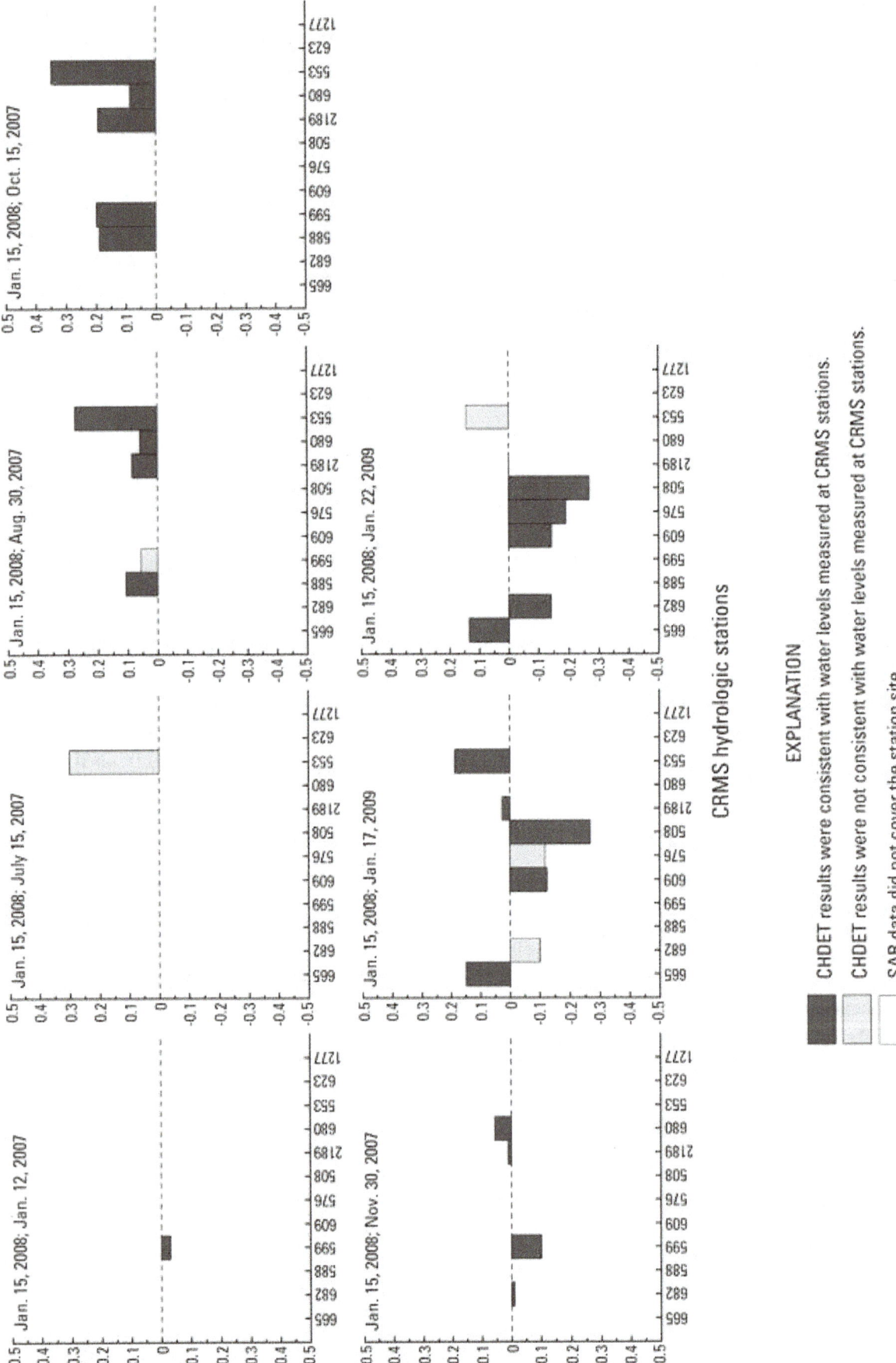

Figure 13. Change-detection (CHDET) of inundation results compared with water-level measurements at inland hydrologic stations within the Coastwide Reference Monitoring System (CRMS). PCI image processing software was used to identify changes between the reference- and target-Synthetic Aperture Radar (SAR) scenes that represented inundation on the target scenes (PCI, 2007; Ramsey, Werle, and others, in press). The Phased Array type L-band Synthetic Aperture Radar (PALSAR) scenes were acquired by the Japanese Aerospace Exploration Agency's Advanced Land Observing Satellite. (Dates provided are acquisition dates of reference scene [first] and target scene [second]; please see tables 10 and 11 for associated data). *A*, Results for the western coastal region. *B*, Results for the eastern coastal region.

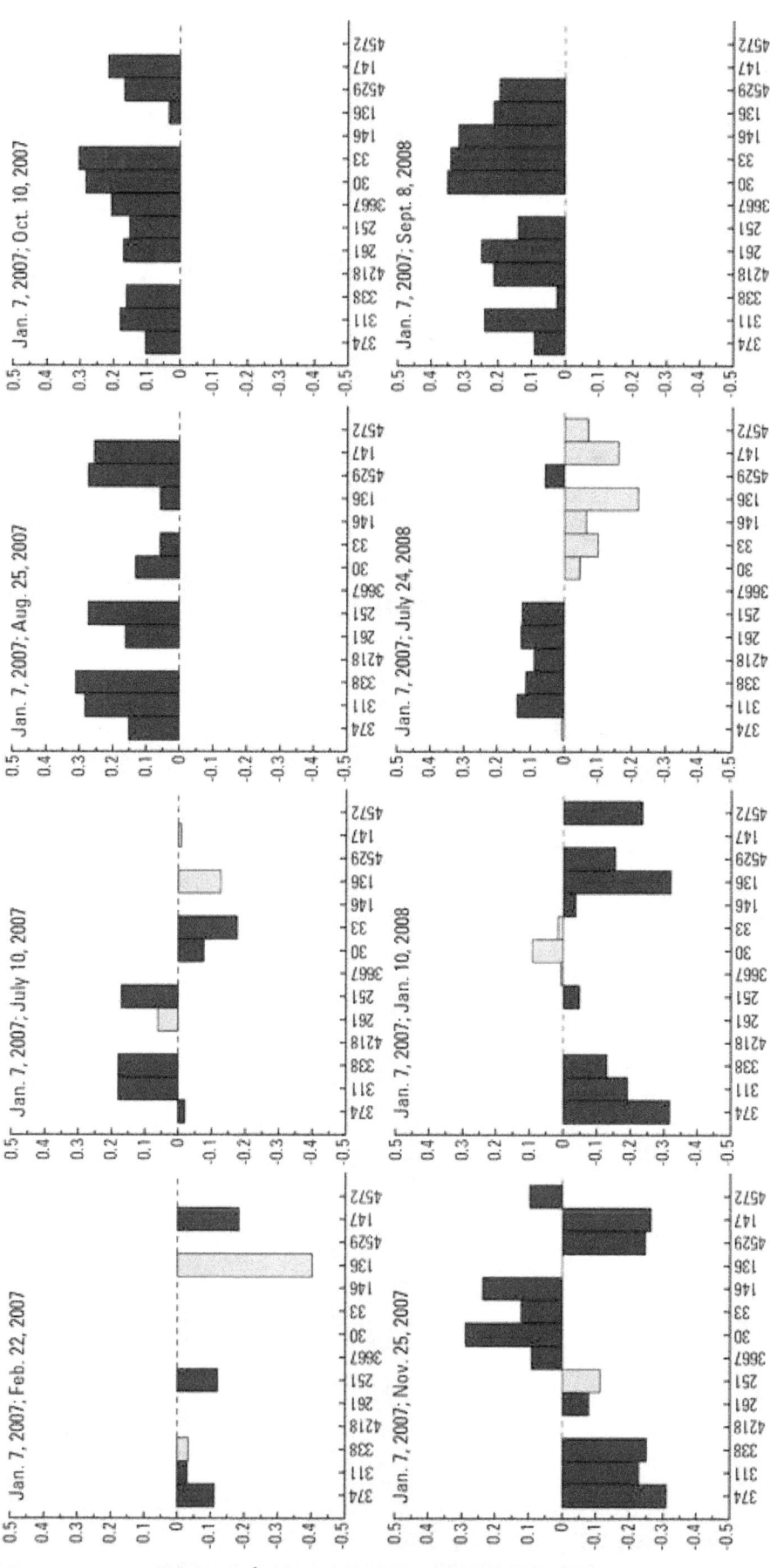

Figure 13.—Continued   Change-detection (CHDET) of inundation results compared with water-level measurements at inland hydrologic stations within the Coastwide Reference Monitoring System (CRMS). PCI image processing software was used to identify changes between the reference- and target-Synthetic Aperture Radar (SAR) scenes that represented inundation on the target scenes (PCI, 2007; Ramsey, Werle, and others, in press). The Phased Array type L-band Synthetic Aperture Radar (PALSAR) scenes were acquired by the Japanese Aerospace Exploration Agency's Advanced Land Observing Satellite. (Dates provided are acquisition dates of reference scene [first] and target scene [second]; please see tables 10 and 11 for associated data). *A*, Results for the western coastal region. *B*, Results for the eastern coastal region.

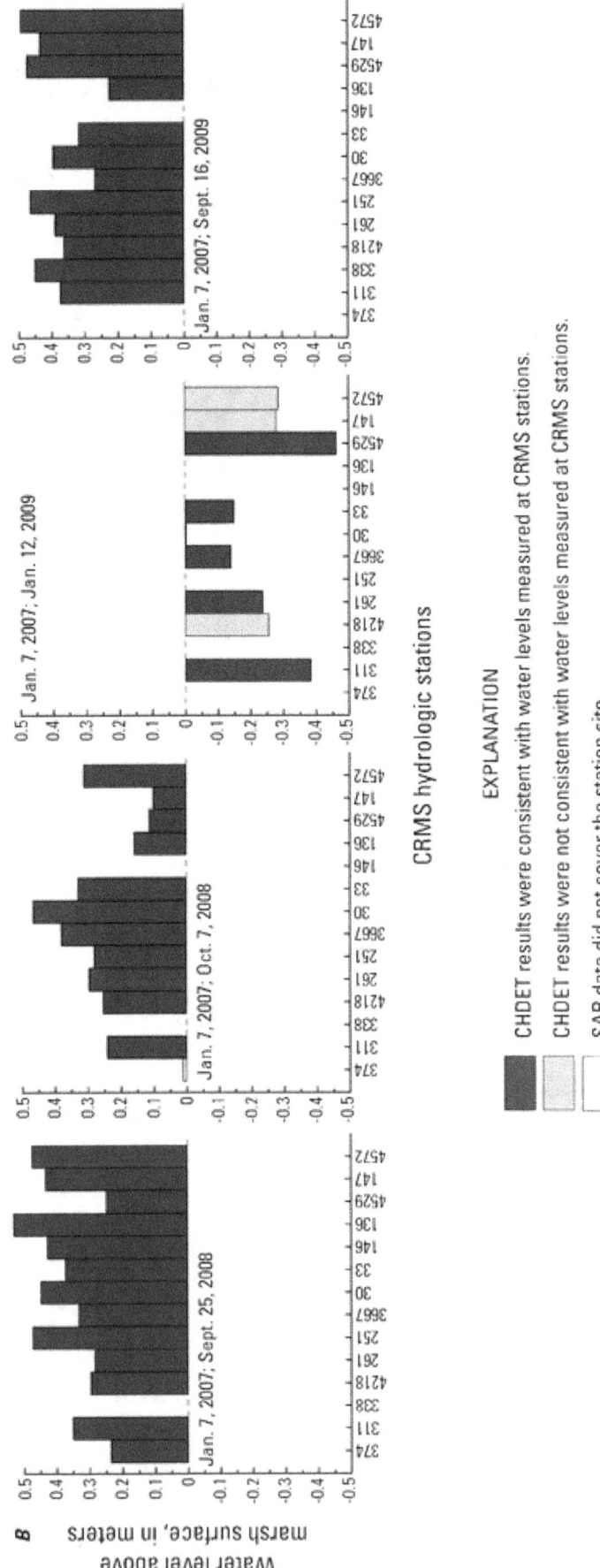

Figure 13.—Continued Change-detection (CHDET) of inundation results compared with water-level measurements at inland hydrologic stations within the Coastwide Reference Monitoring System (CRMS). PCI image processing software was used to identify changes between the reference- and target-Synthetic Aperture Radar (SAR) scenes that represented inundation on the target scenes (PCI, 2007; Ramsey, Werle, and others, in press). The Phased Array type L-band Synthetic Aperture Radar (PALSAR) scenes were acquired by the Japanese Aerospace Exploration Agency's Advanced Land Observing Satellite. (Dates provided are acquisition dates of reference scene [first] and target scene [second]; please see tables 10 and 11 for associated data). *A*, Results for the western coastal region. *B*, Results for the eastern coastal region.

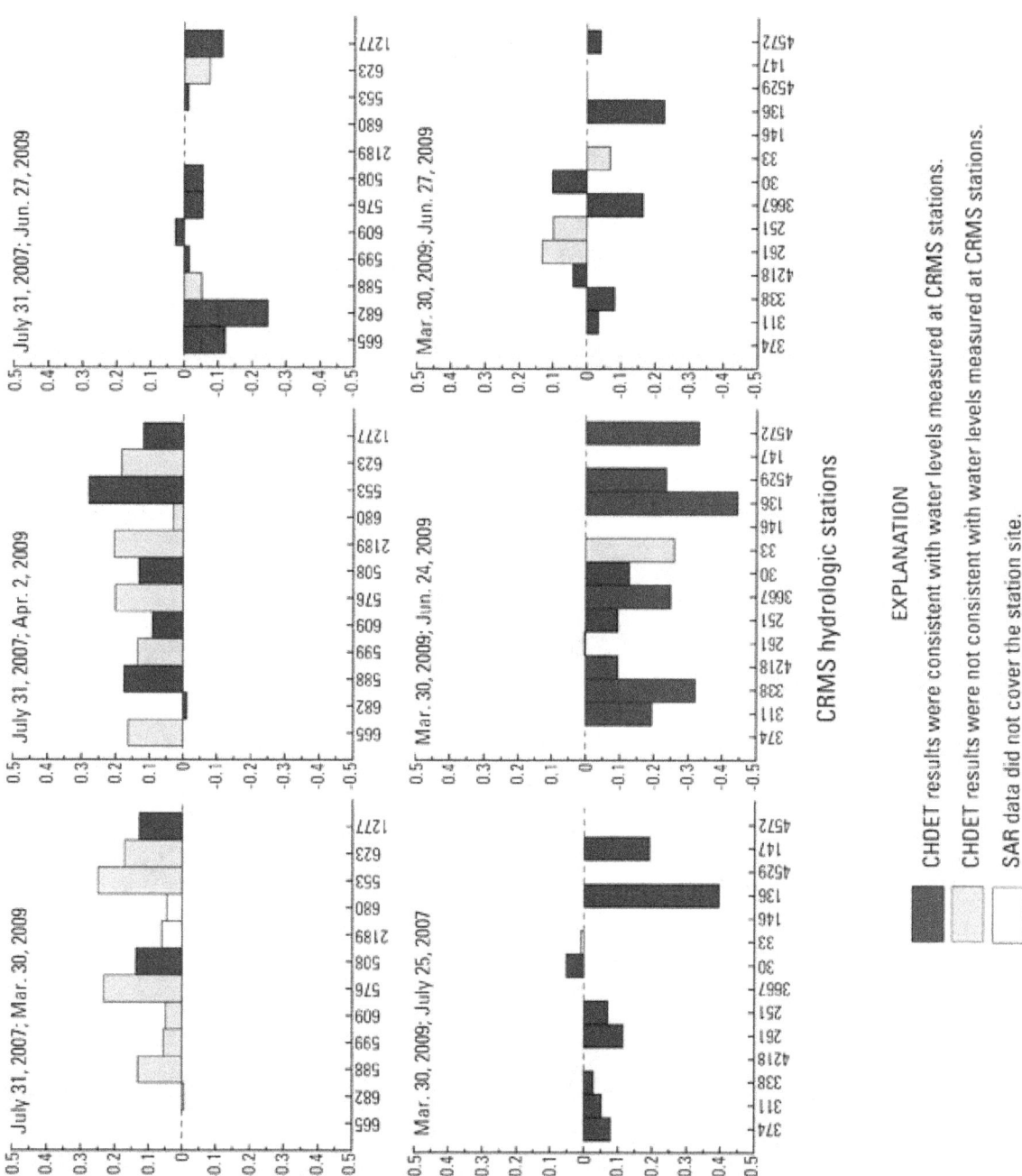

Figure 14. Change-detection (CHDET) of inundation results compared with water-level measurements at inland hydrologic stations within the Coastwide Reference Monitoring System (CRMS). PCI image processing software was used to identify changes between the reference- and target-Synthetic Aperture Radar (SAR) scenes that represented inundation on the target scenes (PCI, 2007; Ramsey, Werle, and others, in press). The Advanced Synthetic Aperture Radar (ASAR) scenes with horizontal transmit and receive polarization were acquired by the European Space Agency's Envisat satellite. (Dates provided are acquisition dates of reference scene [first] and target scene [second]; please see tables 12 and 13 for associated data). *A*, Results for the western coastal region. *B*, Results for the eastern coastal region.

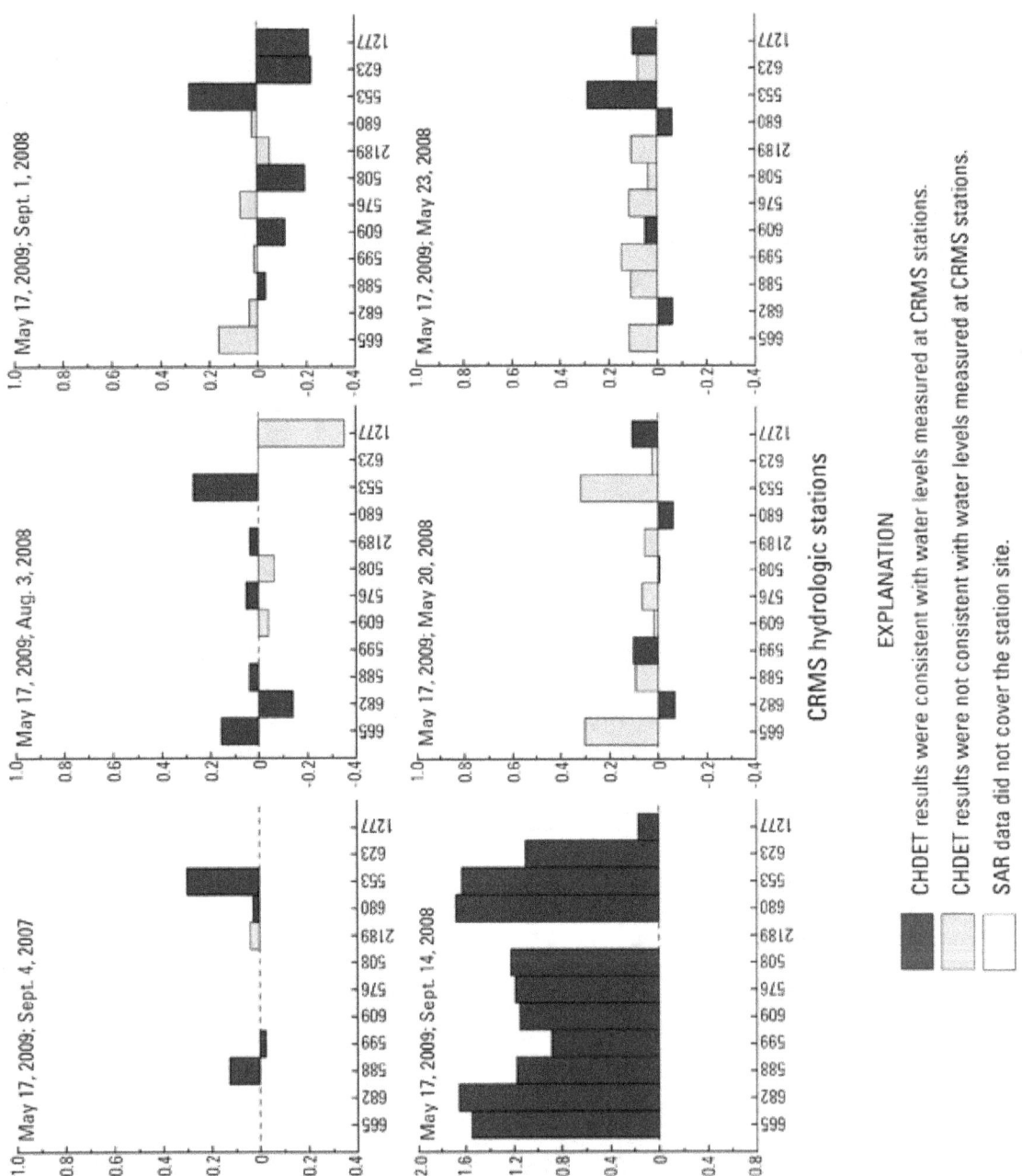

Figure 15. Change-detection (CHDET) of inundation results compared with water-level measurements at inland hydrologic stations within the Coastwide Reference Monitoring System (CRMS). PCI image processing software was used to identify changes between the reference- and target-Synthetic Aperture Radar (SAR) scenes that represented inundation on the target scenes (PCI, 2007; Ramsey, Werle, and others, in press). The Advanced Synthetic Aperture Radar (ASAR) scenes with vertical transmit and receive polarization were acquired by the European Space Agency's Envisat satellite. (Dates provided are acquisition dates of reference scene [first] and target scene [second]; please see tables 14 and 15 for associated data). *A*, Results for the western coastal region. *B*, Results for the eastern coastal region.

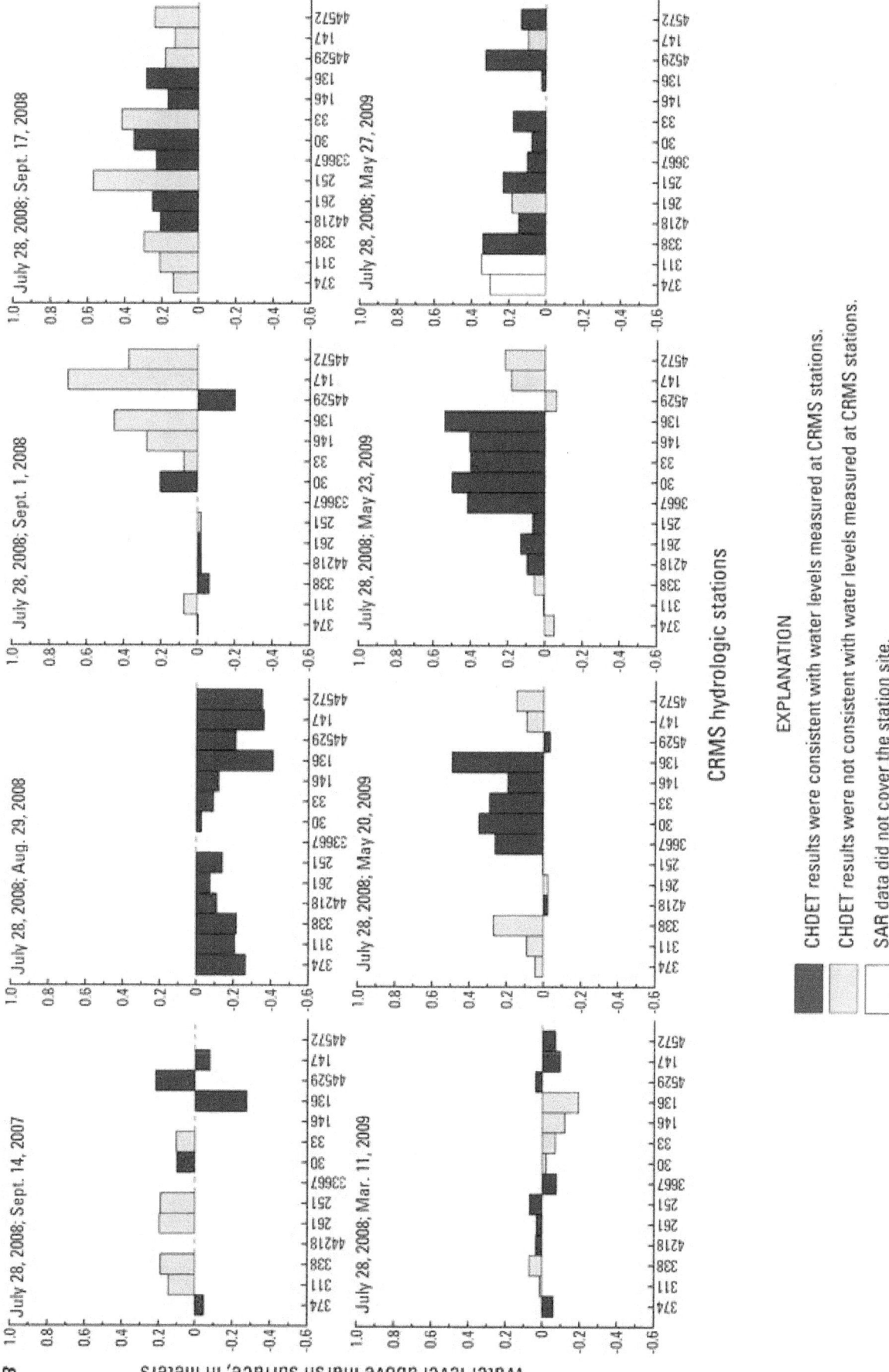

Figure 15.—Continued Change-detection (CHDET) of inundation results compared with water-level measurements at inland hydrologic stations within the Coastwide Reference Monitoring System (CRMS). PCI image processing software was used to identify changes between the reference- and target-Synthetic Aperture Radar (SAR) scenes that represented inundation on the target scenes (PCI, 2007; Ramsey, Werle, and others, in press). The Advanced Synthetic Aperture Radar (ASAR) scenes with vertical transmit and receive polarization were acquired by the European Space Agency's Envisat satellite. (Dates provided are acquisition dates of reference scene [first] and target scene [second]; please see tables 14 and 15 for associated data). *A*, Results for the western coastal region. *B*, Results for the eastern coastal region.

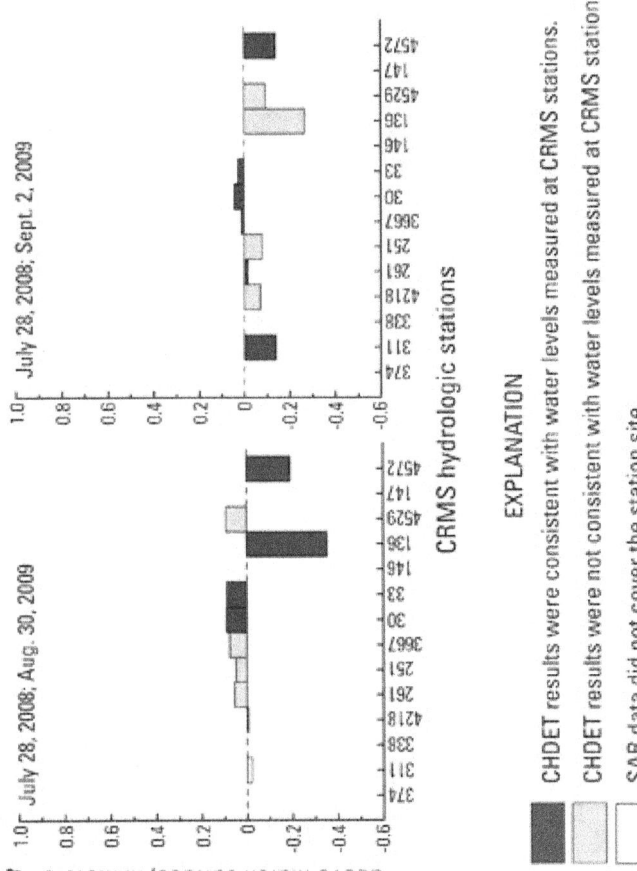

Figure 15.—Continued   Change-detection (CHDET) of inundation results compared with water-level measurements at inland hydrologic stations within the Coastwide Reference Monitoring System (CRMS). PCI image processing software was used to identify changes between the reference- and target-Synthetic Aperture Radar (SAR) scenes that represented inundation on the target scenes (PCI, 2007; Ramsey, Werle, and others, in press). The Advanced Synthetic Aperture Radar (ASAR) scenes with vertical transmit and receive polarization were acquired by the European Space Agency's Envisat satellite. (Dates provided are acquisition dates of reference scene [first] and target scene [second]; please see tables 14 and 15 for associated data). *A*, Results for the western coastal region. *B*, Results for the eastern coastal region.

Conclusion

PALSAR-based inundation mapping performed consistently and exhibited high correspondence with inland water-level recordings, whereas ASAR-based mapping performed poorly to marginally, only improving to adequate performance rates when water levels were well below or above marsh-surface height over extensive areas throughout a scene. Overall, Phased Array type L-band SAR (PALSAR) based inundation mapping was the most successful resulting in higher than 83 percent correspondence with the presence and absence of inundation as recorded at inland hydrographic sites. Inundation mapping derived from C-band Advanced SAR (ASAR) was less successful with overall correspondences with inland recordings around 60 percent. Exceptions to the low performance of ASAR-based inundation mapping occurred when water levels were well below or above ground, occurring over spatially extensive portions of the ASAR scene.

Full assessment of ASAR-based inundation mapping was hindered by paucity of appropriate reference scenes. This paucity resulted from abnormally high sea levels in 2007 and 2008 that increased the complexity of choosing reference scenes collected during times of minimum flooding. The use of a consistent set of reference selection criteria and thresholds related to inundation determination promoted inundation mapping but did not completely overcome the low performance of ASAR-based inundation mapping. Many factors contributed to lower performance of ASAR-based mapping in terms of correspondence of maps with inland water-level records; some examples of those factors include highly variable coverages and look directions (ascending or descending orbits) leading to variable local incident angles from scene to scene. An added complexity was what seemed to be an increased sensitivity of (C-band) ASAR to progressive changes in the look angle from far to near range as compared to (L-band) PALSAR.

Results of the current study suggest that mapping of coastal inundation at high temporal frequency is highly successful when using PALSAR data. PALSAR and ASAR data are both useful but are most beneficial when collected within the constraints of a predetermined strategy; however, a problem is presented by a lack of availability of data. If data availability were overcome, PALSAR and ASAR data could be combined with ground-based field measurements to better define variable canopy-structure influences on inundation mapping performance. Furthermore, coupling SAR collections with satellite-based optical image collections (such as by Landsat Thematic Mapper) could improve inundation mapping, including detection of subcanopy inundation, as well as further development of water-level change mapping and canopy-structure mapping. An integrated system for satellite data collection will also provide for rapid emergency response, strategic resource management, and resource science advancement.

References

Alaska Satellite Facility, 2010, The MapReady Remote Sensing Tool Kit, version 2.3.6: Fairbanks, Alaska, Alaska Satellite Facility, accessed September 27, 2010, at www.asf.alaska.edu/sardatacenter/softwaretools.

Chabreck, R.H., 1970, Marsh zones and vegetative types in the Louisiana coastal marshes: Baton Rouge, Louisiana State University, Ph.D. dissertation, 112 p.

Coastal Louisiana Ecosystem Assessment & Restoration, 2006, Enhancing landscape integrity in coastal Louisiana—water, sediment & ecosystems, 3 p., accessed September 27, 2010, at http://www mvd.usace.army.mil/lcast/pdfs/CEM2.pdf.

Committee on Earth Observation Satellites, 2008, The earth observation handbook, climate change special edition 2009–2010, accessed September 27, 2010, at http://www.eohandbook.com.

Dobson, M.C., Pierce, L.E., and Ulaby, F.T., 1996, Knowledge-based land-cover classification using ERS-1 / JERS-1 SAR composites: IEEE Transactions on Geoscienceand Remote Sensing, v. 34, no. 1, p. 83–99.

European Space Agency, 2007, Envisat ASAR product handbook, issue 2.2, available online at http://Envisat.esa.int/handbooks/asar/.

Fisher, J.I., and Mustard, J.F., 2007, Cross-scalar satellite phenology from ground, Landsat, and MODIS data: Remote Sensing of Environment, v. 109, p. 261–273.

Fisher, J.I., Mustard, J.F., and Vadeboncoeur, M.A., 2006, Green leaf phenology at Landsat resolution—Scaling from the field to the satellite: Remote Sensing of Environment, v. 100, p. 265–279.

Grings, F.,Ferrazzoli, P., Karszenbaum, H., Tiffenberg, J., Kandus, P., Guerriero, L., and Jacobo-Berrles, J.C., 2005, Modeling temporal evolution of Junco marshes radar signatures: IEEE Transactions on Geoscience and Remote Sensing, v. 43, no. 10, p. 2,238–2,245.

Hager, Brad, Brakenridge, Bob, Eichelberger, John, Hunsaker, Carolyn, Killeen, Tim, Zhong, Lu, Parrish, Jay, Pichel, Bill, Turcotte, Don, Woodward, Nick, Dobson, Craig, Sauber, Jeanne, Moghaddam, Mahta, Ramsey, Elijah, Holt, Ben, Blom, Ronald, Huberty, Brian, Glasscoe, Margaret, Clemente-Colón, Pablo, and Brooks, Ben, 2009, Hydrological and ocean applications, in Report of the DESDynI Applications Workshop October 29–31, 2008, UC Sacramento Conference Center: Pasadena, Calif., National Aeronautics and Space Administration, Jet Propulsion Laboratory, California Institute of Technology, p. 33–56, accessed on August 26, 2011, at http://desdyni.jpl.nasa.gov/applications/.

Henry, J.B., Chastanet, P., Fellah, K., and Desnos, Y.L., 2006, Envisat multi-polarized ASAR data for flood mapping: International Journal of Remote Sensing, v. 27, no. 10, p. 1,921–1,929.

Hess, L.L., Melack, J.M., Filoso, S., and Wang, Yong, 1995, Delineation of inundated area and vegetation along the Amazon Floodplain with the SIR-C synthetic aperture radar: IEEE Transactions on Geoscience and Remote Sensing, v. 33, no. 4, p. 896–904.

Hong, Sang-Hoon, Wdowinski, S., and Kim, Sang-Wan, 2010, Evaluation of TerraSAR-X observations for wetland InSAR application: IEEE Transactions on Geoscience and Remote Sensing, v. 48, no. 2, p. 864–873.

Kasischke, E.S., Smith, K.B., Bourgeau-Chavez, L.L., Romanowicz, E.A., Brunzell, Suzy, and Richardson, C.J., 2003, Effects of seasonal hydrologic patterns in south Florida wetlands on radar backscatter measured from ERS-2 SAR imagery: Remote Sensing of Environment, v. 88, no. 4, p. 423–441.

Kiage, L.M., Walker, N.D., Balasubramanian, Shreekanth, Babin, Adele, and Barras, John, 2005, Applications of Radarsat-1 synthetic aperture radar imagery to assess hurricane-related flooding of coastal Louisiana, International Journal of Remote Sensing, v. 26, no. 24, p. 5,359–5,380.

Klemas, Vic, 2005, Resolution requirements for coastal applications of new geostationary satellites, in Proceedings of the 14th Biennial Coastal Zone Conference, New Orleans, La., July 17–21, 2005: U.S. National Oceanic and Atmospheric Administration, Coastal Services Center, 5 p., accessed August 19, 2011, at https://www.csc noaa.gov/cz/CZ05_Proceedings/pdf%20files/Klemas.pdf.

Klemas, V.V., Dobson, J.E., Ferguson, R.L., and Haddad, K.D., 1993, A coastal land cover classification system for the NOAA Coastwatch Change analysis project: Journal of Coastal Research, v. 9, no. 3, p. 862–872.

Lang, M.W., Townsend, P.A., Kasischke, E.S., 2008, Influence of incidence angle on detecting flooded forests using C-HH synthetic aperture radar data: Remote Sensing of Environment, v. 112 p. 3,898–3,907.

Leconte, R., and Pultz, T., 1991, Evaluation of the potential of Radarsat for flood mapping using simulated satellite SAR imagery: Canadian Journal of Remote Sensing, v. 17, p. 241–249.

Lewis, A., F. Henderson, and D. Holcomb, 1998.Radar fundamentals—The geoscience perspective, in Henderson F., and Lewis, A., eds., Principles and Applications of Imaging Radar: New York, John Wiley and Sons, p. 131–181.

Louisiana Oil Spill Coordinator's Office (LOSCO), 2007, Louisiana GIS digital map of May 2007: Baton Rouge, La., Office of the Governor, Digital Versatile Disc.

Lunetta, R.S., Lyon, J.G., Guindon, Bert, and Elvidge, C.D., 1998, North American landscape characterization dataset development and data fusion issues: Photogrammetric Engineering and Remote Sensing, v. 64, no. 8, p. 821–829.

Lu, Zhong, and Kwoun, Oh-ig, 2008, Radarsat-1 and ERS InSAR analysis over southeastern coastal Louisiana—Implication for mapping water-level changes beneath swamp forests: IEEE Transactions on Geoscience and Remote Sensing, v. 46, no. 8, p. 2,167–2,184.

Matgen, P., Schumann, G., Henry, J.B., Hoffmann, L., and Pfister, L., 2007, Integration of SAR-derived river inundation areas, high-precision topographic data and a river flow model toward near real-time flood management: International Journal of Applied Earth Observation and Geoinformation, v. 9, no. 3, p. 247–263.

Moghaddam, M., McDonald, K., Cihlar, J., and Chen, Wenjun, 2003, Mapping wetlands of North American boreal zone from satellite radar imagery, in Geoscience and Remote Sensing Symposium, IGARSS '03, Toulouse, France [Proceedings]: New York, NY, IEEE Press, p. 261–263.

Morton, R.A., Bernier, J.C., Barras, J.A., and Ferina, N.F., 2005, Rapid subsidence and historical wetland loss in the Mississippi Delta Plain—Likely causes and future implications: U.S. Geological Survey Open-File Report 2005-1216, 124 p.

National Oceanic and Atmospheric Administration, 2010, Tides & currents: National Oceanic and Atmospheric Administration's National Ocean Service, accessed September 27, 2010, at http://tidesandcurrents.noaa.gov/index.shtml.

Neyland, R., 2007, The effects of Hurricane Rita on the aquatic vascular flora in a large fresh-water marsh in Cameron Parish, Louisiana: CASTANEA, v. 72, no. 1, p. 1–7.

Nielsen, C., and Werle, D., 1993, Do long-term space plans meet the needs of the mission to planet earth?: Space Policy, v. 9, no. 1, p. 11–16.

Ormsby, J.P., Blanchard, B.J., and Blanchard, A.J., 1985, Detection of lowland flooding using active microwave systems: Photogrammetric Engineering and Remote Sensing, v. 51, no. 3, p. 317–328.

PCI Geomatics, 2007, Geomatica User Guide: Richmond Hill, Ontario, Canada, PCI Geomatics Enterprises Inc., 179 pp.

Pope, K.O., Rejmankova, Eliska, Paris, J.F., and Woodruff, Robert, 1997, Detecting seasonal flooding cycles in marshes of the Yucatan Peninsula with SIR-C polarimetric radar imagery: Remote Sensing of Environment, v. 59, no. 2, p. 157–166.

Ramsey, E.W., III, 1995, Monitoring flooding in coastal wetlands by using radar imagery and groundbased measurements: International Journal of Remote Sensing, v. 16, no.13, p. 2,495–2,502.

Ramsey, E.W., III, 1998, Radar remote sensing of wetlands, in Lunetta, R.S., and Elvidge, C.D., eds., Remote sensing change detection—Environmental monitoring methods and applications: Ann Arbor, Mich., Ann Arbor Press, Inc., p. 211-243.

Ramsey, E.W., III, 2005, Remote sensing of coastal environments, in Schwartz, M.L., ed., Encyclopedia of Coastal Science—Encyclopedia of Earth Sciences Series: Dordrecht, The Netherlands, Springer, p. 797–803.

Ramsey, E.W., III, Laine, S., Werle, D., Tittley, B., and Lapp, D., 1994, Monitoring Hurricane Andrew damage and recovery of the coastal Louisiana marsh using satellite remote sensing data, in Wells, P.G., and Ricketts, P.J., eds., Proceedings of the Coastal Zone Canada '94—Cooperation in the coastal zone, v. 4: Dartmouth, Nova Scotia, Canada, Coastal Zone Canada Association, Bedford Institute of Oceanography, p. 1,841–1,852.

Ramsey, E.W., III, Lu, Zhong, Rangoonwala, Amina, and Rykhus, Russell, 2006, Multiple baseline radar interferometry applied to coastal landcover classification and change analyses: GIScience Remote and Sensing, v. 43, no. 4, p. 283–309.

Ramsey, E.W., III, Lu, Z., Suzuoki, Y., Rangoonwala, A., and Werle, D., 2011, Monitoring duration and extent of storm surge flooding along the Louisiana coast with Envisat ASAR data: IEEE Journal of Selected Topics in Applied Earth Observations and Remote Sensing, v. 4, no. 2, p. 387–399.

Ramsey, E.W., III, Nelson, G., Baarnes, F., and Spell, R., 2004, Light attenuation profiling as an indicator of structural changes in coastal marshes, in Lunetta, R.S., and Lyon, J., eds., Remote Sensing and GIS Accuracy Assessment: New York, NY, CRC Press, p. 59–73.

Ramsey, E.W., III, Nelson, G., Sapkota, S., Laine, S., Verdi, J., and Krasznay, S., 1999, Using multiple polarization L band radar to monitor marsh burn recovery, IEEE Transactions on Geoscience and Remote Sensing, v. 37, no. 1. p. 635-639.

Ramsey, E.W., III, Spruce, J., Rangoonwala, A., Suzuoki, Y., Smoot, J., Gasser, J., and Bannister, T., in press, Monitoring wetland forest recovery along the lower Pearl River with daily MODIS satellite data: Photogrammetric Engineering and Remote Sensing.

Ramsey, E.W., III, Werle, D., Lu, Z., Rangoonwala, A., and Suzuoki, Y., 2009, A case of timely satellite image acquisitions in support of coastal emergency environmental response management: Journal of Coastal Research, v. 25, no. 5, p. 1,168-1,172.

Ramsey, E.W, III, Werle, D., Suzuoki, Y., Rangoonwala, A., and Lu, Z., in press, Limitations and potential of optical and radar satellite imagery to monitor environmental response to coastal emergencies in Louisiana, USA: Journal of Coastal Research.

Richard, K., Brown, D., and Rhome, J., 2006, Tropical Cyclone Report Hurricane Rita 18–26 September 2005: National Oceanic and Atmospheric Administration, National Hurricane Center, accessed August 19, 2011, at http://www.timothyhorrigan.com/documents/hurricane/TCR-AL182005_Rita.pdf.

Sasser, C., J. Visser, E. Mouton, J. Linscombe, and S. Hartley, 2008. Vegetation types in coastal Louisiana in 2007, U.S. Geological Survey Open-File Report 2008-1224. Atlas: The Louisiana Statewide GIS. LSU CADGIS Research Laboratory, Baton Rouge, LA, 110, http://atlas.lsu.edu

Schaber, J., and Badeck, F., 2003, Physiology-based phenology models for forest tree species in Germany: International Journal of Biometeorology, v. 47, p. 193–201.

Smith, L.C., 1997, Satellite remote sensing of river inundation area, stage, and discharge—A review: Hydrological Processes, v. 11, p. 1,427-1,439.

Strategic Online Natural Resources Information System, 2009, SONRIS Integrated Applications: Louisiana Department of Natural Resources, accessed August 18, 2011, at http://sonris-www.dnr.state.la.us/www_root/sonris_portal_1.htm.

Töyra, Jessika, and Pietroniro, Alain, 2005, Towards operational monitoring of a northern wetland using geomatics-based techniques: Remote Sensing of Environment, v. 97, p. 174–191.

Wang, Yong, 2004, Seasonal change in the extent of inundation on floodplains detected by JERS-1 Synthetic Aperture Radar data: International Journal of Remote Sensing, v. 25, no. 13, p. 2,497–2,508.

Werle, Dirk, Martin, T.C., and Hasan, Kahled, 2000, Flood and coastal zone monitoring in Bangladesh with Radarsat ScanSAR—Technical experience and institutional challenges: Johns Hopkins APL Technical Digest, v. 21, no. 1, p. 148–154.

Publishing support provided by
the Lafayette Publishing Service Center